4.13.78

STUDIES IN MARXISM, Vol. 1
Proceedings of the First Midwest Marxist Scholars Conference

MARXISM
and
New Left Ideology

**Ileana Rodríguez and
William L. Rowe, Editors**

MARXIST EDUCATIONAL PRESS
Minneapolis

Copyright © 1977 Marxist Educational Press
All rights reserved.

First printing 1977

Printed in the United States of America

Library of Congress Catalog Card Number 77-085850

ISBN 0-930656-00-8(series)
ISBN 0-930656-03-2(vol. 1, Hardcover)

Marxist Educational Press
c/o Department of Anthropology
University of Minnesota
224 Church Street S.E.
Minneapolis, Minnesota 55455

2011187

CONTENTS

Introduction: First Midwest Marxist Scholars Conference   7

Eduard Batalov and the Philosophy of Revolt: The New Left through Soviet Eyes   9

    Ileana Rodríguez

The Rise of the New Left   27

    William Simbolov

Marxism, Revisionism, and the State   43

    Terence Ball

Science as a Science   53

    Erwin Marquit

Public Sphere, Labor, and Interaction: A Methodological Critique of Jürgen Habermas' Social Theory   71

    Robert Holub, Wigand Lange, Sara Markham Pietsch, Stephen Pietsch, Charles Spencer, and Ronald Young

New Left Theories on the Mode of Production   95

    Domenico Sindico

INTRODUCTION: FIRST MIDWEST MARXIST SCHOLARS CONFERENCE

A conference on "Marxism and New Left Ideology" sponsored by the Minnesota Marxist Scholars was held November 20-21, 1976, in Minneapolis at the University of Minnesota. About fifty persons, mostly faculty and graduate students from universities in Minnesota, Wisconsin, and Iowa, attended the sessions.

The conference was an outgrowth of the increasing interest in Marxism among academic workers in the region. The source of this growing interest is, no doubt, the fact that Marxism is not a rigid dogma, but continues to develop with the development of the world.

As the chief weapon of the proletariat in its struggle for emancipation, Marxism has always come under pressure from the bourgeoisie, which uses its control over the means of mental production to wage ideological warfare against Marxism from without and to encourage petty-bourgeois elements in their attempt to transform Marxism into an ideology against itself by replacing its revolutionary content with a reformist spirit on the one side and a pseudo-revolutionary ultra-leftism on the other. Marx himself commented on such efforts to misdirect the movement bearing his name with his classic remark to Lafargue: "What is clear is that I myself am not a Marxist."

The fact that Marxism is not a dogmatic, closed system, but continues to develop, makes it difficult for one first becoming acquainted with Marxism on the academic level through the growing number of journals or professional society caucuses of Marxist orientation to distinguish among the various ideological groupings represented there. Such groups include: (1) those who consciously borrow a restricted range of ideas and methods from Marxism; (2) those who supposedly accept most of the "spirit" of Marxism, but see what they regard as significant errors and oversights by the founders of Marxism — in particular, Marx, Engels, and Lenin; (3) those who consider themselves as creatively developing Marxism, but do so on the basis of erroneous assessments of the developments of the world or lack of understanding of the materialist conception of history; and, finally, (4) those who continue to develop Marxism along the main lines of its founders.

The conference on Marxism and New Left Ideology was convened with the purpose of seeking sources of misunderstanding of Marxism and differences with Marxism among representatives of the first three groups above who can be roughly associated with the term "New Left." If there was a dominant ideological current shared by most (although not by all) participants in the conference, it can perhaps be characterized as follows: recognition of materialist dialectics as the logic of nature, society, and thought; recognition of the working class and, in particular, its industrial core, as the principal revolutionary force in the developed capitalist countries; recognition of the essential content of the international class struggle as the struggle between the forces of international monopoly capital on the one side and an alliance of forces on the other, the main elements of which are the workers of the developed capitalist countries along with progressive sectors of the petty bourgeoisie, the anti-imperialist forces of the developing countries, and the peoples of the socialist countries.

EDUARD BATALOV AND THE PHILOSOPHY OF REVOLT:
The New Left through Soviet Eyes

Ileana Rodríguez
University of Minnesota

1. Introduction

Eduard Batalov's book, *The Philosophy of Revolt*,[1] introduces us to a Soviet Marxist view of that multi-dimensional phenomenon of the 1960s generically known as "The New Left." The book opens the Marxist theory of the period to a dimension of criticism unknown or ignored in the West, that of the more advanced thinkers in the socialist countries.

Although Batalov's work aims at a complete comprehension of the New Left, the focus of attention is on Herbert Marcuse, with turns toward Sartre, Fanon and Debray for the New Left tendencies Marcuse cannot cover. New Left predecessors like Erich Fromm and C. Wright Mills come into play, and some other directions are explored; but in general the Frankfurt School predominates, while Charles Reich and Theodor Roszak are taken to represent more recent developments. Thus the configuration of certain major strains in recent U.S. critical theory gradually emerges.

To the degree that the book brings together the intellectual production of the advanced capitalist and the socialist countries, its presentation and critique must be situated on three levels:

Batalov's comprehension and examination of the texts he cites, his own political orientation, and the adequation and interpretation of the versions of Marxism put forth by the group Batalov represents and the group he studies. While the groups have their own politics, naturally each one's view of Marxism involves a critique of political theory aimed at transforming reality. What is achieved here is the meeting of two Marxisms in order to highlight agreements and disagreements and thus re-establish a dialog that was interrupted and deformed by the Cold War and the McCarthy years.

The most polemical level is that of the reading and interpretation of New Left texts because it is here that the group's partisan view of Marx surfaces. On many occasions Batalov's reading seems deliberately mal-intentioned and tendencious, and New Left weaknesses and lapses seem exaggerated. But Batalov's hyperbole accomplishes an indispensible function of ideological clarification. With his strategy of simplification and caricature, his main differences with the New Left emerge, in relation to the orientation articulated by Marx in his last thesis on Feuerbach.

The book points out the non-proletarian and petty-bourgeois base of the New Left, and the structural changes this base has undergone (Batalov notes that New Left intellectuals have been called theorists of the "urban middle classes in revolt"); in addition, an analysis is made of several specific questions that serve as touchstones to this group: the category of negation with its two variants, the "Great Refusal" and the "Dialectic of Negation"; the role of technology and its concomitants; the various totalitarian tendencies of the new stage of capitalism; consumerism and its effects; the denial of the proletariat's revolutionary character; the radical role of students and intellectuals; the romanticization of Third World countries, and the emphasis on the peasantry as a revolutionary group; the championing of spontaneity and violence as tactics; and finally, the idea of Utopia.

Batalov does not ignore the divisions and peculiarities of the heterogeneous political groupings that came to be known as the "New Left," and he has decided to accept the designation in question because it brings together the most important elements that served to form the consciousness and political tendencies characterizing a significant social sector. But Batalov does distinguish between those groups which stress culture and enlightenment — that is, the critical theorists — and those which are dedicated to radical politics, primarily of a Third World orientation. He believes that the New Left's historical emergence is a consequence of the crisis of capitalist reaccommodation after two world wars.

New Leftists are confronting four important political forces: the technocrats, the right wing, the liberal bourgeoisie and the Old Left, which the new group believes to consist of Social Democrats and Communists. Their primary target is the bourgeois "establishment," and all those social groups and political parties that have integrated themselves into the state monopoly system and have thus lost their "revolutionary spirit."

2. *The Dominant Traits of the New Left*

Batalov adheres to an apparently normative, or "classical," interpretation of Marxism, and from this point of view, he selects the most significant traits, the most constant concepts and the most open contradictions of New Left theorists.

The world view of the New Left is preoccupied with the image of disintegration operating on all levels — moral, political, cultural. This world view has its tie with consumption and technology, which have united as the basis for a totalitarian society in which "technological rationality" and "voluntary submission" have replaced the force of bayonets to create an integrated proletarian class.

Starting with this undifferentiated supposition, the New Leftists suggest the creation of a new world by a new man, who, serving as the agent of history, produces new social relations based not on domination and subjugation, but on the full expression of "creative human nature."

The matter, so set forth, has two basic requirements: to identify a new historical subject, able to serve as the vehicle for this necessary task of historical creation, and to find a theory able to provide the basis for this subject's education and coming to consciousness. Many New Left factions believed they had found their historical agent in marginal groups, ethnic minorities, students and intellectuals, and in Third World peoples; and they believed they had found their theory in a particular interpretation of Marxism.

A series of paradoxes issue from such beliefs, two of which emerge with particular force. The groups mentioned are revolutionary because they are marginal — i.e., either because they lack access to consumption, or, like most of the students, because they reject, or claim to reject, the world of consumption. The proletariat in the developed countries is not revolutionary for the opposite reasons: It has, and wishes to have still more, access to consumption. The first contradiction emerges when a group asserts that material needs are not the only ones that motivate the militant revolutionary trends in Third World countries and those groups identifying with them: There are also spiritual needs — those associated with the terms, alienation, lack of power, creativity and self-determination — that constitute the motor force of anti-capitalist protest. But, curiously enough, consumerism only affects the proletariat in an negative way, while it leaves other groups (the big bourgeoisie excluded, of course) virtually pure in their discontent and revolutionary aspirations.

If the Third World fulfills certain revolutionary needs for New Left theorists, they also need certain indigenous theorists able to articulate the relations between Third World militancy, the passivity of workers in the developed countries and Marxist theory. It is in this context that such theorists do in fact emerge.

But New Left thinkers, in both advanced and underdeveloped countries, take from Marxism only what is useful for themselves, as a counter-theory denoting the destruction of the power structure; the elements in existing society that Marxists see as positive are identified as signs of capitulation to the bourgeoisie and are thus rejected. There are three dominant ways in which the New Left sees Marx: One tries to complete Marxism with social theories invented by bourgeois social scientists; another contrasts some aspects of Marx with others — e.g., economism versus humanism; a third divides Marx from Engels, or Marx from Lenin.

3. *Evaluation of the New Left: Three Perspectives*

Batalov presents at least three interpretations of the radicalism of the '60s and early '70s. The most simplistic flourishes in the camp of the bourgeois social sciences. Here, the decade of protests is a mystery made clear only in terms which are without true meaning or value, such as "youth rebellion," "sexual development," or "generation conflict." Bourgeois theorists turn to these physiological or psychological explanations and never base their findings on an analysis of capitalist society, when, in fact, it is only with such an analysis that one could uncover the roots of those contradictions out of which the protest movement actually emerges.

The second interpretation comes from the very center of the New Left itself. From this point of view, the protest is not a by-product, but the essential product of the age. The recent wave of radicalism is said to signal a new stage of capitalism, in the midst of which a generation of militant youth is replacing the proletariat as the new agent of history. Further, since the New Leftists do not, nor are about to, constitute an independent class, they have difficulty in defining their socio-political position, and, as usually happens in such cases, they appropriate and identify with the functions that characterize other, already existing social groups or classes. Thus, while they deny the revolutionary potential of the proletariat, they identify with it, but because they prize their own "revolutionary" ideas as having exclusive validity, they are quick to specify the differences in class consciousness which separate them from the working class.

It should suffice to point out the abyss across which the New Leftists hoped to leap with these identifications, but this identification process leads to the New Left characteristic which Batalov criticizes most: their utopianism.

The third interpretation is Batalov's. According to him, the radical protests emerge as an expression of the collision between an older industrial civilization and a newer technological-scientific one which is in the process of being born. The protests incarnate the inevitable price Western society pays for its entry into a "technetronic, post-industrial" era in which the capitalist framework of relations becomes increasingly narrow. The Soviet critic, then, agrees with the New Left in their view of a change of stages, but does not agree to the corollary the new stage is supposed to imply. For him, the militant aspects of the proletariat change historically, but do not disappear. The accelerating appearance of newer and newer forms of productive development leads to what Batalov calls the "cognitive barrier" between generations. By this he means that at times it is difficult to distinguish the new forms of proletarian militancy. The technical revolution, which shortens the time between innovation and its production for mass consumption that generates new life-styles, is the origin of the world of things in which a generation develops and experiences rapid change. Though the effort is often unsuccessful in consumer society, young people in each new generation attempt to construct their own language, their own sub- or anti-culture; so, in the same way, each new generation of workers tries to resolve its own problems.

The true source of the radical protests of the '60s is found in the two dominant tendencies of contemporary society: the radical change in the social function of science, and the narrowing of the human base needed for the reproduction of bourgeois relations. These two characteristics significantly affect the position of intellectuals: They lose the relative freedom they enjoyed in not seeing themselves directly tied to the production of surplus value, and in not being the direct object of control and domination. Now social changes have left a surplus of intelligence: The intellectual is converted into a proletarian of intellectual labor and is directly employed in material production.

In their current dilemma, the intellectuals are no longer bourgeois, but are not yet proletarian. Batalov coins a new term of doubtful semantic standing: The intellectual is a *lumpen bourgeois*. Students increasingly find themselves veering toward this status, and gradually join the swelling ranks of the surplus intelligentsia.

Finding their class position fluid and ever decaying, intellectuals have recourse to their *metier* which allows them to elaborate a theory that elucidates their situation and expresses their protest. For a moment, anarchism fills the requirements, because it stresses only the negative features of criticism and gives support to the destructive side of the revolutionary process, without retaining anything positive. Thus it expresses the ideology of a group which has not yet crystallized and which has not been able to find a solution to the dilemma which confronts it.

In a short, summary history, Batalov shows how, since the 19th century, anarchism has been the reaction of the petit bourgeoisie in the face of the growing role of the state, and he cites Lenin to reinforce his thesis, since Lenin sees anarchism as the product of desperation. Anarchism attracts those who, in an effort to rectify the loss of their privileges, overlook theory and rely on the spontaneity of action. Thus, the New Left, situated between two stages of capitalism and two class positions, remains locked into two polar categories: anarchism and utopianism.

4. Marcuse and Batalov: Four Concepts

In direct opposition to the New Left's somber views that posit the imminent disintegration of society, Batalov notes that the statistics of the '60s show a relatively stable world. True, there is war and a war economy, but these feed a high and rising level of production.

At the same time, this is also the period in which the idea of integration begins to show its illusory character.

Trapped in the dilemmas created by consumption, the New Left develops a theory of society based on the conception of a unitary and closed capitalist world. Marcuse, who most fully articulates this view, describes a society in which the submission of the subject to the whole is practically absolute; technology has come to dominate capitalist relations, and the designated historical agent of Marxist theory is left without any space for action and is confounded by "one-dimensionality."

This term comes to be synonymous with the absence of social forces of opposition and criticism that can submit the system to their negation; it implies a total reconciliation with the *status quo*. For this reason the problem of consciousness acquires primary importance, as does the idea that proletarians and managers, united by consumption and mass media, have lost their peculiar, distinctive character.

Within this schema, the basic question lies in determining the role of technology in the system and the degree of human tolerance or resistance possible in the current processes of production, distribution and consumption.

As a first answer, Marcuse puts forth the idea of the "Great Refusal." Even with all its qualifications, this idea is for Batalov little more than a reformulation of Adorno's "negative dialectics," in which only the total negation of society expresses the possibilities for rebellion and change. Marcuse indicates that the Marxist dialectic does not take into account the changes that have occurred today and underestimates the possible forces of integration. Because of this internal rigidity without spaces, Marcuse believes that only external action on the system can constitute a source of fundamental qualitative change, as it is projected from beyond the confines of the antagonistic opposites which bind the closed system. This is the context which gives Third World movements their importance for the New Left and its theorists.

Adorno takes issue with the Hegelian "dictatorship of concepts," which he finds present in most Marxist constructs. Situating himself on a level even more radical than Marcuse's, he is at odds with the idea of any sort of integral system. For him, everything is always in movement, and he proposes to destroy concepts and lay bare their contradictions. He also wishes to emphasize the perpetual thesis and anti-thesis of things, even at the expense of excluding any possible synthesis. This universalization of contradictions — and, significantly, Batalov finds a similar conception in

Mao — is Adorno's way of shaking off sleeping and integrated consciousness; it is, from his perspective, the best theoretical basis for analyzing reality.

The theorists of the New Left in the Third World concur with Adorno-style negation; hence they reject Western culture, deny class differences in capitalist countries, and continue believing in the power of criticism against bourgeois structures.

With reference to the lack of proletarian militancy in the developed countries, we have already noted how Marcuse attributes this phenomenon to the way consumerism and mass media create a set of false needs that manipulate the class consciousness of the proletariat to the point of integrating it. According to Marcuse, consumption levels the needs of workers and managers, and by closing the abyss that separates the two classes, it negates the dynamics that impel class struggle.

Batalov shows that, for all its apparent sophistication, Marcuse's theory is ultimately mechanistic and reductionist. The satisfaction of material needs becomes the motor of class struggle; this struggle seemingly absent, one must identify those poor and dispossessed groups that can restore the dynamism to history. We have already seen who these groups are supposed to be. Since they are cut off from the processes that, according to classical Marxism, would lead them toward revolutionary consciousness and action, it follows that a basic New Left tenet must be that of a radical rupture with false needs in order to create true ones. Hence the unilateral emphasis on negation is confirmed by tautology.

Batalov does not fail to recognize Marcuse's sharpest insights into the material and cultural tendencies of capitalism, but he does not concede that bourgeois society has arrived at its point of saturation. He pinpoints the paradoxical nature of New Left arguments in their identification of social integration with disintegration. Here the New Left takes up the liberal bourgeois view of preserving the *status quo*; integration, although alienated, is said to draw militancy from the worker and perpetuate immobility. But it is false to believe that economic integration leads automatically to political and social integration, and that a fusion of workers and capitalists has taken place.

In his refutation of the New Left's class analysis, Batalov becomes most critical. As a classical Marxist, he affirms that sociological study must be based on production and not the circulation and consumption of commodities. If consumption presupposes production — and Marcuse always refers to technology and its effects — this does not guarantee that worker and capitalist needs are the same. A genuine equalizing process assumes a qualitative change in the system and the transition from capitalism to socialism.

The satisfaction of vital needs does not eliminate the production of surplus value, or private ownership of the means of production. Even if vital needs are satisfied, other secondary needs remain: The demand for culture and self-determination impels the struggle for disalienation and political power. Even conceding the empirical value of Marcuse's analysis, Batalov criticizes the New Left for assuming that capitalist successes are permanent and that the system will no longer have crises. Marcuse overlooks the qualitative development of those needs created by the very technological transformations he stresses. The new needs only neutralize economic gains, since they are essential conditions for the normal functioning of capitalism. Meanwhile, the gains are compensations for losses that find expression in a greater intensification of exploitation, in an expenditure of mental energy, a diminution of creativity, in a growth rate which finds no equivalent in wage hikes, and in the anxieties generated by productive and social transformations.

Batalov recalls that Marx himself had asserted that with the growth of wealth and productive forces, the worker's situation improves. In 1891, Engels denied the thesis of the progressive and absolute immiserization of the working class, pointing out how growing worker militancy and organization resist immiserization; but Engels was quick to add that such successes do not diminish the insecurity continually plaguing workers. Later, Lenin denied any direct relation between the proletariat's economic impoverishment and its revolutionary potential; rather the latter can develop from the disruption or deterioration of the proletariat's way of life.

Marcuse's formula for revolutionary development is to create new and authentic needs. But this solution should be based in production; otherwise, it is anarchistic and utopian. The new needs do not emerge spontaneously, at the call of the intelligentsia; they sleep in the shadow of the means of production, and only awaken in the process of productive transformation. New cultural and political needs are not separated from older ones; rather new and old interconnect genetically and functionally. The main contradictions impelling transformation are not in the superstructures, although sometimes the struggle appears to be occurring there; the lightest wind of crisis carries apparently superstructural demands to the economic base.

Pessimism and negation are the two faces of Marcuse's theory. His analysis does not emerge from a concrete grasp of the system of dominant relations, but from a speculative conception of the power of the negative dialectic that corresponds to the transitional situation of his own social group. Now we may understand why Marcuse sees Hegel as the philosopher of negation, when, on the contrary, the main point of Hegel is contradiction. Negation is a process and a result; it is the manifestation of the contradiction already resolved. Marcuse's dialectic cannot express or do much to bring about the social transformation which it so partially and inadequately grasps.

For Batalov, changes in class consciousness wrought by new relations are slow in emerging; thus intellectuals do not yet perceive the reality of their changing class situation. But their discontent is patent, and extends beyond the confines of the intellect, to become a manifestation of the revolutionary spirit otherwise peculiar to the classical proletariat. To the degree that the intellectuals' demands do not return to the past, they become proletarian. But the practical activity of the intelligentsia does not deny the conception of the proletariat as a revolutionary force; on the contrary, it nourishes and confirms that conception.

5. *Utopia, Violence, Imagination and Liberty*

The only viable route for transforming reality that the followers of Marcuse propose is constant criticism aimed at realizing all that the capitalist establishment considers utopian. To be utopian, for the New Leftists, is to cross the line between the possible and impossible — to dispense with the obstacles, so that what is repressed may emerge, and thus, to "bring the imagination to power." Since the New Left sees no revolutionary possibilities in the present, the need is for a violent rupture and a leap to a world only thinkable by the most fantastic imaginings. For them there is no possibility of conservation in the negation process, since what is, seems completely barren of socialist possibilities. Instead, the limited and solid extant world must be completely negated, smashed by a violent act that opens out on the plasticity of an inconceivable but possible world that humans can fabricate through revolutionary will and *élan*.

Here, "utopia" is something other than the bourgeois notion of a fantastic place without basis in the historical world. New Left utopianism sets the stage for their notions of plasticity, consciousness and imagination, which connect Marcuse with the views of Sartre and Camus. An objectivistic positivism about the present veers toward an existential-style subjectivism about the future: Liberty is affirmed as the absolute activity of the subject which may project and leap beyond the constraints of what Sartre calls the *practico-inert*.

Together, liberty and imagination may cross the frontiers dividing politics and aesthetics. In social terms, imagination is the means for liberating humanity from a deterministic and positivistic vision of the world; in aesthetics, it is the means for creating beauty and harmony. Utopia is half way between science and art, because the utopian perspective appeals to emotive and imaginative impulses generated in periods of individual exhaustion and pessimism.

A political-aesthetic union emerges, once humanistic relations and social institutions are liberated from the restraints of capitalism. Before this moment, the imagination serves only as a psychological defense mechanism rather than as a revolutionary means for distinguishing the viable from the impossible.

Related to this utopia of political-aesthetic union is the carnival and festive character attributed to the revolutionary process. This is especially the case in the New Left's view of May, '68, and the U.S. student protests. Carnival and rebellion merge in an ecstatic and lurid surrealism. The slightest turn of events reveals the most politically suspect dimensions of the social orgy.

Examined closely, the New Leftist's view of liberated imagination exposes their sectarian and elitist character. They propose liberty for the vanguard, but fear to place it in the hands of the still-sleeping masses. Liberated imagination points toward violence.

New Leftists claim that we live in a totalitarian world where violence structures all aspects of modern life. They distinguish between open violence and a masked form that permits the opposition to act whenever it does not trespass legal limits and menace established power. Democracy creates ill-founded illusions and hopes that ultimately disunite and discourage the opposition: Parliament and law are only mechanisms that catch up the opposition in a bourgeois game that threatens to neutralize their will to revolution.

Given this view of capitalist politics, the only answer to violence is intolerance toward all that is or seems bourgeois, and adulation of all that is marginal and outside the law. Fanon, for example, praises the cathartic power of revolutionary violence, and argues for a change of place between exploited and exploiter. Violence exerts its benevolent power over the consciousness of both oppressed and oppressor: It restores dignity to the oppressed; it leads to a recognition of error by the oppressor. In this way, revolutionary methods are appropriate to the forces from without that will divest the system of its repressive character. Thus, guerrilla fighters represent the truly revolutionary forces; the party that does not dedicate itself to guerrilla warfare is not revolutionary.

The other side of this critique is directed at the Soviet Union and the Socialist countries. The New Left criticizes them for their bureaucratization and the values engendered by competition with the West. They believe that Socialism has been sidetracked; *ergo*, capitalism and Soviet Socialism are one and the same, and the same logic of revolution applies to both.

Batalov recalls how "utopia" has generally evoked images of an ideal social organization, but for him, significant utopian thought leads to a type of action directed toward a specific goal that is possible and rational; and it also denotes the dividing line between the interests of conformative and oppositional groups. Under present capitalist conditions, New Left theorists play a positive role by stressing the possibility of those projects the bourgeoisie wishes to dispose of as utopian, and in emphasizing the importance of going beyond the limits. The existential notion of liberty served a similar function during the Resistance, when the Nazis posed their occupation as inevitable and irreversible. But Batalov shows that New Leftists fail to distinguish between abstract and concrete possibilities, that they abstract and absolutize ideas as applicable to all times and places. The true problem remains without resolution: to define the objective role of liberty and imagination, and to distinguish this from the subjectivistic and arbitrary one theorized by the New Left.

Batalov sees liberty as the product of the interaction between the subject and historical necessity; it is not absolute because it is not exterior to the cognitive process: Its conception of the non-existent is always tied to the existent, which determines and conditions it. It is undeniable that, in relation to the exterior world, its role is that of negation; but as it negates one necessity, it creates another one — precisely so as not to remain in the realm of the utopian. New needs are born in an interaction with ultimate reality; the imaginative process should not have arbitrary goals, but ones which follow the specific objective logic of historical development.

Today high production rates have made possible things that were only utopian yesterday; but this does not mean we can accelerate historical development in order to see our desires fulfilled immediately. If the subjective desire to change reality is not supported by objective conditions, utopian projects are not realistic; consciousness alone is not sufficient, if only because it is not determined arbitrarily by the subject, but by pre-existing objective conditions. Subjectivism, or the lack of objective consciousness, is itself an objective characteristic with which the theorist must contend.

The problem of violence has cultural implications, since the violent act reveals a will to destroy, preserve or develop a cultural inheritance. According to Batalov, the matter exposes the New Left's lack of vision with respect to the correlation of class forces. Certainly in our epoch revolutionary transformations have thus far been carried out by means of violence; and the urgency of transformation is made more patent to the degree that capitalist development continues. But a premature outbreak of violence incites an overwhelming reaction from the right. Necessity, or realism, and non-necessity, or utopianism, must be determined and weighed in an analysis of class alignments and forces.

Reformist tendencies have clearly affected sectors of the working class; but Batalov denies the effort to generalize and eternalize these tendencies and make them the basis for a critique of the CPSU's position on peaceful coexistence that is full of misconceptions and ultimately meaningless. He begins his argument by clarifying the difference between the political implications of "peaceful" pacifism and parliamentarianism, in order to mark out the dividing line between New Left tactics and those he champions.

The New Leftists make a literal interpretation of "peaceful coexistence" and conclude that it implies the negation of revolutionary violence. On the other hand, the bourgeoisie sees revolutionary violence as treason against one's country. For Batalov, both views obstruct the passage to class struggle.

In the face of New Left misconceptions, he takes such notions as "repressive tolerance," "law," and "military force," and demonstrates that while based in reality, they overplay the extent of bourgeois control of the masses. Batalov does not deny that "repressive tolerance" exists, that the law is the expression of the will of the ruling class, or that the military-industrial apparatus is powerful. Such factors help us understand the demand for revolutionary violence, but we should not forget that laws, for example constitute limits to oppression which the proletariat has forced the bourgeoisie to place on the books through arduous and costly battles. On this basis, Batalov roundly opposes the New Left's depreciation of the democratic process. Even where democracy has no real power, and where the space conceded is very narrow, the opposition does not stop seeking and utilizing the legal means of expression available. Such activity prepares the socialist revolution that is born in the transformation of old-style democracy into socialist democracy: The form of the new society is determined by the maturity of the society destroyed.

As for guerrilla warfare, Batalov asserts that seeing this form of struggle as the revolutionary method *par excellence* is a reversion to long-discarded Trotskyist views that today find their correlative in Maoism. Guerrilla warfare is used as a pretense for attacking "Soviet revisionism" and *detente* — even though no other country has been a stronger supporter of guerrilla movements, when they have been determined to constitute a viable mode of revolutionary activity. For Batalov, the New Left's manner of articulating the problem is based on misconceptions of the history of revolutionary movements and on the casual and superficial way the post-war generation sees warlike conflicts. *Detente* is a form of competition between distinct systems and classes on a world-wide level. As such, it submits capitalism to two pressures, the external one of socialism and the internal one of the working class. In *detente*, capitalism risks its profits and its overall system; thus its efforts to regulate the market and permit the intervention of the state: All these, says Batalov, are preliminary steps for the formation of socialism.

Detente favors the liberation of people from imperialism, and helps consolidate socialism; in no way do its advocates subordinate revolutionary wars to their own interests. By way of example, Batalov cites the case of Vietnam.

For the New Left, Vietnam is the locus of guerrilla warfare, the school of revolutionary apprenticeship. The emphasis in New Left analysis goes unilaterally toward the militance of the Vietnamese masses, while the socialist world's military and economic aid and the pressure it exerts over the aggressor are conveniently forgotten or left unspoken. Here, as is the customary case, one aspect of revolutionary practice dominates over the rest, and revolutionary theory born of past experiences continues to be relegated to the bin of dogmatism. In this case, New Leftists reveal their ahistorical and ultimately ignorant view of the past and present of the socialist countries: They see socialism with the eyes of philosophers and moralists, forgetting that if socialism breaks with the previous order, it is born out of it. For the New Left, the ideal socialism is measured with the development of capitalism and is presented as its opposite; if real, concrete socialism does not fill their abstract requisites, they reject it for the same reasons they reject capitalism.

Finally, Batalov asks, what is the idea of the future and the "New Man," and what are the New Left's plans for implementing this idea? For him, the New Left mentors perceive a new world in the distance — a happy or anti-world, in which the utopian "New Man" frees himself from work by converting it into play. The theorists do not elaborate how this world will come to emerge in the midst of present-day capitalism. On the contrary, this happiness tends to create islands within bourgeois society; such are the hippies in communes and cooperatives before their commercialization. While having no direct relation with the New Left, the hippies are very close to them in attitude and behavior. Obviously, the communal island is viable for a small sector of capitalist society, but it is not so for the masses involved in material production and trapped in daily routine.

The organizational principles of the new society are collective property, control and distribution: This is the model of Marcuse. Roszak's model elaborates a combination of heterogeneous elements adequate to everything: artisanal, medium and heavy industry, self-regulated and non-exploitative activity, anti-bureaucracy, the coordination of the industries controlled by workers. Everyone speaks out against organization because the pariah of bureaucracy is associated with it. Certainly, says Batalov, the bureaucracy is one of the most vulnerable aspects of capitalism; it extends its power to all parts of the social organism — e.g., the augmentation of the military bureaucracy and its concentration of power. Further, capitalist bureaucracies are united to national institutions, to factories, etc.: To destroy the bureaucracy is equivalent to destroying the administrative apparatus of the state. Under socialism, however, the point is not to destroy but to reorganize the administrative apparatus because it organizes and sustains social life.

Conclusions

The Philosophy of Revolt has all the virtues of the most serious academic investigation. By examining the most salient traits of New Left theory and praxis during their most fruitful years, Batalov evinces an effort to study his subject critically, but not without sympathy. He fully concedes that New Left theorists produced a telling empirical assessment of the sixties. But for the reasons cited above, the New Left is seen as so trapped by the immediacy of their situation that they may only think about future possibilities for change in utopian terms. Batalov attempts to set New Left theory "back on its feet." While his concurrences with it are frequent, his differences are extensive and fundamental, and the perspective of our own present enables us to see that he is more totalizing and historical.

Batalov's method is to take those aspects best defining the New Left and push them toward their extreme logical limits. He then shows that the innovative concepts of the New Left cannot survive the thrust of a rigorous Marxist analysis. First, a view of capitalism based on consumption and technology falsifies class relations and negates class struggle; second, an emphasis on negation and violence distorts the nature of the revolutionary process — it is inclined unilaterally toward the destructive and disregards the constructive; third, a utopianism projected beyond concrete possibilities posits a historical trajectory that is illusory and improbable; fourth, a unilateral and undifferentiated view of the socialist countries negates the positive influence and pressure they exert on international revolutionary movements.

In all this, Batalov would seem to be correct. Nevertheless, his book has deficiencies that cannot be left unnoticed. While we insist that Batalov is more fully historical than most New Left theorists, we must still contend that he underplays history for the sake of a critique of theory, and he too readily identifies New Left concepts with the ideology of the group they represent. He sometimes confuses constructs necessitated by the discursive method with the reality those constructs only approximate. Thus, for example, his emphasis on Marcuse duplicates the very problem he criticizes: Just as not all capitalist countries are the same, neither are all New Leftists. Marcuse is highly representative, but he is not the only New Left thinker — nor can Sartre, Fanon and Debray round out the picture. In fact, Batalov's critique cannot be considered as truly opposed to all of the New Left, since many important aspects of his attack on Marcuse's lack of class analysis coincide with certain recent re-evaluations emanating from sectors of the New Left itself. Batalov's perspective on the future positive development of particular New Left strains would have probably been different if he had dealt with Lucien Goldmann and the New Working Class theorists of France and Italy, instead of with figures so unrepresentative of the best of the New Left as Reich and Roszak.

We can point to a related but still more important instance of our point in Batalov's approach to the historical context in which the New Left emerges. A more adequate analysis of the group would have to account for the fact that it represents the most progressive members of a generation that grew up in the McCarthyist fifties — those who succeeded in conserving at least part of their critical power. The McCarthyist context is one of the sources for the New Left stress on negation and criticism, and the group cannot be fully understood without a rigorous scrutiny of the impact of the repression and anti-Communist propaganda so prevalent in the Cold War period. That the New Left theorists turned to radical, but non-Communist intellectuals who developed their theories under the sway of European Fascism and World War II is a fact that needs careful exploration. A historical comprehension of the origins of the generation first articulating those ideas that culminate in New Left theories would throw light on the class situation and ideological possibilities of the student rebels of the sixties. A better hold on the future evolution of New Left ideas and the groups generating them could only emerge from an analysis that is more ready than Batalov's to deal with those political affinities and antipathies mediating between a group's economic situation and its praxis. In this respect, Batalov is unable to grasp the historical irony in the New Left's greatest single accomplishment: that its overtly anti-Soviet leftism served as the ideology for a mass movement ultimately helpful to national liberation movements which drew their primary material support from the Soviet Union.

Batalov handles New Left anti-Sovietism too gingerly. He fails to penetrate its sources and thereby only gives us a partial view of its consequences. The result is an inadequate theorization of those developments that in one case have led certain New Leftists to join with the Communist Party in the Common Program for France, and that in the wake of Angola and the Italian elections, pave the road for a slow but noticeable turn toward the Old Left by the New, in many parts of the capitalist world.

But in writing this book, Batalov does confront at least one significant cause and effect of this aspect of New Left ideology: their general ignorance and misreading of the socialist countries. It is absolutely essential to know the historical reality of these countries to enter into the debate over socialism. It is not enough to construct models and then judge reality by them. But that is what New Left utopianism leads to. Batalov opposes that utopianism with sound arguments which demonstrate the power and vitality of critical thinking in the socialist world.

By translating books like *The Philosophy of Revolt*, Progress Publishers open a true dialog between socialist thinkers and those progressive groups who struggle against capitalist forces in their very centers of power.

NOTE

1. Eduard Batalov, *The Philosophy of Revolt: Criticism of Left Radical Ideology* (Moscow: Progress Publishers, 1975).

THE RISE OF THE NEW LEFT

William Simbolov

1. Introduction

Only historical analysis can distinguish and relate the theorists who supposedly articulated New Left practice, and the broad numbers who, having read and understood New Left theories or not, were identified as New Left. One problem is the seemingly radical content of New Left theories in conjunction with an often feeble and purely theoretical practice; another is the sometimes valuable if anarchistic tactics of New Left activists, coupled with their frequent lack of theory, beyond spontaneous "humanistic" outrage against repression, racism, violence and exploitation. If New Left theory is often contradictory and unsystematic, it has sometimes set off sparks and generated conceptions useful to later Marxist theorization and action. On the basis of often misguided or partially grasped assumptions, New Left activists have accomplished limited but praiseworthy tasks in the struggle against imperialism and racism, especially in the anti-Vietnam War movement; they have pointed toward new possibilities, potential alliances and means of struggle against advanced capitalism, and have helped to break through the Marxist quarantine in post-McCarthyist America.

But their exaggerated revolutionary expectancy, their extreme acts and reflexive anti-communism have fed the general political apathy, and the confusion about Marxism, which recent capitalist crises have been manipulated to encourage.

For some, New Left spontaneity led to a reverse need for theory, which resulted in fetishizing Marxism as a politically neutral mode of intellectual dissent, more and more the province of a small intelligentsia. For others, spontaneity merged with anti-Soviet feelings to generate a need for party that could only be served by pseudo-Leninist groups which alienate potential Marxist sympathizers and feed ultra-left alliances with reaction — all in the name of some "pure socialism." In many ways, the New Left has created an ineffectual locus for people awakening to the fact that the source of their discontent lies in capitalism. An intellectualist reaction to chaotic activity feeds elitist feelings that widen the gulf between Marxism and those sectors vital to its realization.

But because our ultimate concern is with those often well-intentioned sectors who were called New Left and those who may yet come to Marxism through New Left theory which now so dominates what goes under the name of Marxism in the universities, we should stress certain positivities. Starting with Marx, many of the most forceful fighters against capitalism began as discontented radicals filled with petty-bourgeois idealism and only later brought to more viable ideas. In their development, even their ill-founded conceptions had progressive contours. Before any contribution of New Left theory or activism can serve the movement toward socialism, it must be subjected to a historical criticism which accounts for what New Leftists see correctly (but partially), and what they are unable to see at all.

Our ultimate effort must be to negate the New Left's regressive tendencies, to win over the most reasonable and progressive of those who are and may become New Left, at least to seeing that they should ally with the world movement toward socialism as the best political means to work for the struggles they most believe in.

This strategy should have meaning in Western Europe and the United States, where many are realizing the utopian dead ends toward which extreme New Left theory leads, and where world events, in Vietnam, Chile, Portugal, Angola, and now South Africa may be combining to create a new climate of understanding and rapprochement among the most reasonable members of various sectors of the Left.

2. The Genesis of the New Left

The sources for New Left theory are found in the utopian socialists, the Left Hegelians and the anarchists. The utopians announced the theme of socialism, but failed to base their conception on a comprehensive analysis of society and history, which included a theory of how this socialism was to emerge, except through human will, teleology or moral imperative. The Left Hegelians were also utopians who struck out at existing society in the name of creative idealism. They stressed the theme of alienation and the need to act against it toward a higher human destiny. While the young Marx already saw economic inequality and the capitalist labor process as sources of alienation, he still had not grasped the concrete basis for alienation, and the struggle against it. He found them in the theory of surplus value and the theory of the falling rate of profit. Unable to ground their analysis of the social misery they opposed, the early forerunners often saw causes in surface phenomena. Thus the anarchists urged a leap to new social relations through the destruction not of capitalism, but of the state — even a socialist state able to prevent the return of the very conditions giving rise to capitalist political forms. For Marx and Engels, the capitalist state supported bourgeois relations; in time the socialist state could "wither away," but for this to occur, society had to be kept on a socialist road through the "dictatorship of the proletariat." But while Marx and Engels set forth a program for analyzing the state and other ideological institutions and forms, they never fully elaborated it.

This later became a problem for Marxists. Was the state a mere reflection of economic relations? Why did different capitalist countries take on different political forms? Why could capitalism proliferate different ideologies? Why did archaic forms of consciousness persist under new conditions? How did these and other factors give specificity to given struggles? The answers of "uneven development" and "relative superstructural autonomy," are suggestive of a theory that awaited further development.

Unable to follow the lead of Marx and Engels in this direction, Second International thinkers reduced Marxism to economic determinism. New ideas, new conditions were generated by new economic relations. A party simply kept politics and ideology in line with these conditions: Party "success" could only slightly speed up an inevitable revolutionary process. Yet, since revolution did not seem to come, since the proletariat seemed to slide toward trade union reformism, Second Internationalists sought to append a

Kantian moral dimension to their Marxism — one which led humans to seek a socialist world beyond given conditions. Thus a narrow materialism breeds a return of idealist utopianism.

The extreme sum of these distortions is the revisionism of Eduard Bernstein, who asks the International to give up revolutionary pretensions and to see that the proletariat is not a revolutionary force. Kautsky could not convincingly oppose Bernstein: Only Luxemburg and Lenin could.

These two figures rebel not only against Bernstein, but against Kautsky and company. Lenin saw that the proletariat's potential could not be grasped within the conceptual framework of the Second International. His theories of imperialism and the vanguard party lead to a new global Marxism, and a new view of proletarian action to win and develop socialist state power.

But even on the Second International Left, a division grows. Luxemburg's *Accumulation of Capital* provides some of the keys for imperialism, but her theories of the mass strike draw too much from anarcho-syndicalist tendencies which are ultimately defeating. Lenin wanted workers' democracy, he saw the clear value of strikes, but he did not believe revolution possible through self-managed proletarian development. Workers' uprisings could only lead to revolution through a party able to direct developing proletarian energies and forge alliances with other discontented sectors. Thus, just as Lenin opposes the Revisionists, he opposes leftwing extremists. Just as he opposes economic determinism and reductionism, he opposes theories which overemphasize voluntarist or spontaneous movement toward revolution.

Lenin attacks ultra-leftism in his *Left Wing Communism, an Infantile Disorder*,[1] a basis for communist answers to future Left radicals. But Lenin sought not only to attack. He attempted to make valuable revolutionaries like Luxemburg recognize the validity and necessity of his position.

We stress Luxemburg because, while seen in the thirties as a predecessor of Trotskyism, her emphasis on ideology, workers' control and the as yet undeveloped aspects of Marxism make her an apt predecessor of certain New Left trends.[2] More directly, Luxemburg strains the economistic seams of the Second International, and foreshadows that refashioning of Marxism accomplished by Lenin and the three "Hegelian Marxists" of the 1920s, Korsch, Gramsci and Lukács.

The developing Russian Revolution capped off World War I's socio-economic devastation, to generate an explosion of left culture and thought, and an increasing return to dialectics. The Revolution ended Second International political and theoretical hegemony. In Lenin's work, in the writings of the Hegelian Marxists, a theorization for new circumstances emerges: Objective and subjective bases for present failures and future possibilities of revolutionary consciousness come to the fore. New Left theorist Paul Piccone spells out the major contributions of the three leading Hegelian Marxists to the development of New Left perspectives.[3] Involved in the council movements of 1919, they saw their socialism as the antidote to the post-war revolutionary crises, and aimed their sharpest words against fellow Social Democrats for vulgarizing and deactivating Marxist theory. Their primary bequeathal to the New Left is their opposition to the Second International's crisis theory: the view that capitalism was heading toward an economic cataclysm that would result in socialist revolution. When crises had come to sectors of post-War Europe, they had produced the workers' councils, but not revolution.[4] One reason was capitalist material force, but another was inadequate politicization of the workers. This raised questions about the relation between their own consciousness and political organization. Lenin had shown that revolution could not come through sheer economic force; ideology and activity were bound, and their relation to the economy was mediated by politics and culture. The Second International had succumbed to bourgeois positivism; economism could not integrate a theory of active consciousness. Luxemburg's theories also expressed this narrow determinism, even if they implied the workers' ability to go beyond opportunistic leadership. Lenin's vanguard was recognition of the problem, but the question of mediation still needed elaboration.

The theories of the Hegelian Marxists reflected the aspirations and failure of the workers' councils. For Korsch, the problem of revolution was to break through ideological mediations to generate a society of self-conscious subjects running their own lives free from determination from above. Gramsci explained Western revolutionary failures as resulting from the proletariat's unawareness of its objective interests. Culture did not reflect immediate material conditions, but impeded a translation from social being to consciousness. Thus culture was the main arena in struggle for political hegemony. Socialism was not just a restructuring of property and productive relations, but a total social rebirth through the proletariat's massive politicization and acculturation. Lukács reinterpreted Marxism through the Hegelian dialectic of whole and part, recasting the prevalent bourgeois theme of alienation in the logic of capitalist production. Authentic existence was impossible under capitalism: A split between culture and life was intensified by commodity fetishism which extended a dehumanizing and fragmenting rationality from production to ideology and everyday life, so that even Social Democracy had not escaped. Only the proletariat could grasp the totality beyond reification and could serve as a historical agent of change.

All three figures stressed the development of "collective subjectivity, representing the leap into a new age and the fulfillment of emancipatory dreams" that were influenced as much by the Left Hegelians as by traditional Marxists.[5]

An altered socio-historical context revealed their many theoretical limitations as it blighted hopes for immediate revolution. The post-war processes of social reconstruction led to a defeat of the council movement and the theories it generated; they systematically altered the objective conditions that seemed suitable to collective subjectivity. Still faced with strong worker opposition, capitalism turned to powerful economic and political forces to divert or crush worker discontent and action. The assembly line and the scientific organization of production reduced possibilities for consciousness and self-management. The state began to intervene in production, to control social life through increased bureaucratization and the beginnings of the culture industry. As Fascism emerged, as Europe rushed toward a depression that would lead to Nazism, the Hegelian Marxists could no longer expect proletarian activity to emerge out of the labor process or out of broader cultural mediations. All three leading figures had to focus on immediate political counterforces.

Korsch saw no alternative to new relations in the Third International; he left the German CP in 1926. Gramsci had chosen the communist movement but was imprisoned and killed by the fascists. Lukács traded his theory of ultimate emancipation for the discipline of a coordinated international organization hopefully able to surmount the present impasse and bring about, however gradually, the pre-conditions for the world he sought.[6]

What Piccone fails to underscore is that two of these three Hegelian Marxists, ancestors of the New Left, are decisive figures in Communist history. If we identify much of their work with the New Left, we are only heeding certain tendencies and not others. Hegelian Marxism represents a trend persisting among European Communists even through the thirties and forties. Only certain elements of Hegelian Marxism are developed by the immediate predecessors of the New Left. In a one-sided way, they develop thematics that are common Marxist heritage; under the sway of capitalist hegemony, they coopt many Marxist themes for anti-communist purposes. Hence the early Marx is one-sidedly opposed to the later, and alienation theory is given an existential or Freudian twist to serve as an anti-communist tool. The development of alienation theory by communists (and they were the first publishers and disseminators of the 1844 Manuscripts) is thus pushed into the background, while the distorted uses of this theory meant that Marxists themselves refused to use or emphasize it, thus leaving the field open to further misconstruction.[7]

In effect, New Left theory is in many ways the distorting vessel for many genuinely Marxist themes de-emphasized and left undeveloped in the period dominated by the need to fend off Nazism and then Cold War vilification. Thus our need to take up and recuperate these suspended themes, to restore their proper bases for adequation.

Nowhere is this matter more evident than in the case of Lukács, who so influences the Frankfurt School and who, even more than Gramsci, expresses the bifurcation of Hegelian Marxism toward and away from the world revolutionary movement.

Lukács formulated his views as he moved from a radical stance close to Luxemburg, toward one more in accord with Lenin. By a protracted intellectual maneuver, capitalist reification was seen as a prior stage to the proletariat's transcending its reified real consciousness and its movement, in relation to the vanguard party, toward its potential totalizing consciousness, which would emerge with a socialist adequation of subject and object.

This is the total arc of Lukács' thought in the late 1920s. *History and Class Consciousness* is only a punctuation point in the process, one marked by many positions Lukács would later come to reject. Thus in one essay, "Orthodox Marxism," Lukács developed views that dominate New Left thought; the notion that every single aspect of Marx's theory could be banished, but Marxism would still remain, because it is the method for grasping dialectical relations. On this basis, Lukács attacks Engels' view that human dialectics were based on a dialectics of nature. For Lukács, this is pure mechanistic reductionism, since what distinguishes human from natural relations is the subject-object interaction which is basic to the Marxist dialectic. By attempting to ground this dialectic in nature, Engels makes a metaphysics of Marxism, makes it a positivistic, reified science, which reduces Marx to Feuerbach and reduces activity to the passive response of material forces working through humans. For the early Lukács, then, the gravest political shortcomings of the Second International flow from or are justified by this unhuman dialectics, which Lenin rescues in his political thought and action, but which he still succumbs to in his view of science and epistemology.[8]

This is the Lukács the New Left appropriates and dovetails with an early non-positivistic, non-economistic Marx. But it is Lukács himself who repudiates, as he develops Engels' approach to the ultimate economic determination of culture and art.[9]

Not that Lukács threw out all of his theory: The critique of reified consciousness under capitalism remains in his most "orthodox" writing in the thirties up to the time of his death. Thus his contrast between abstract (Utopian) and concrete possibility:[10] While abstractly anything was possible, concretely only those thoughts were viable which were adequate to potentially dominant tendencies in social reality. This careful dialectic of real and potential remains a Communist heritage.[11]

The non-Communist followers of the Hegelian Marxists also modified Lukács, but in a different direction. The negative critique of the materialism of Engels is extended to Lenin's politics. In fact, the Frankfurt School opposed direct political uses: Party reduced the dialectic, negated the independent power of criticism. The Frankfurt School denied Lukács' unity of social being and consciousness, denied the identity of the proletariat as the unequivocal subject of history, denied any identity between party and proletariat, and party or proletariat with ultimate truth. What they accepted was Lukács' emphasis on reified consciousness, which they developed to explain shifts in capitalism from production to the market, the family and the institutions of domination, authoritarianism and instrumental reason. This reification theory was used mainly to show how alienation came to dominate the proletariat itself, and to account for the emergence of authoritarian patterns which they saw directly in Germany and which they believed had come to dominate the USSR.

The twin disillusion marked by the rise of Hitler and Stalin characterized every aspect of critical theory, and domination as independent of production became their point of theoretical departure. When economic crisis came to sectors of Europe, not socialism but fascism emerged. To Frankfurt School members, the rise of fascism was not explicable by "orthodox Marxism," nor did Soviet views of Nazism indicate any theoretical superiority over other approaches. Russian socialism did not seem a viable alternative to the fascism it was deemed unable to explain or contain. The fear of fascist repression and pessimism about socialist or New Deal state intervention marked the Frankfurt School's theoretical concerns, their intense interest in mediating psychic structures, etc. Their very repulsion to standard bourgeois positivism and standard Marxism led to their most characteristic speculations. Their twin disillusion and their notion of an increasingly closed, managed and instrumentalized totalitarianism which could only be fought by the most radical negations (and hence not really fought at all) charged every aspect of their thinking and constituted their bequeathal to New Left theory.

3. The New Left and Political Ideology

But what were the circumstances of the advanced capitalist world, particularly in the United States, which created a radical force and which, as ideologues hungered for theories suitable to their situation, turned them toward the Hegelian Marxist tradition?

First, much of the Frankfurt School's later theoretical elaboration occurs on U.S. soil; increasingly, critical theory came to see the United States as the prime model for capitalist development.[12] In the fifties, with the rise of irrationalist dissent to the post-War reconstruction, ex-Frankfurt School members trumpeted neo-Marxist interpretations of Freud and Sartre and fed the early Marx into a cauldron of anti-institutional "humanist" revolt. Marcuse's *One-Dimensional Man* joins liberal and "radical" studies of conformism. As a Sartrean reaction to Frankfurt School negativity received theorization in Eastern Europe and France, Marcuse gradually fell in line. Only a radical spontaneous praxis (one inaccessible to workers) could leap through the closed one-dimensional world.[13]

This development seems to mesh with the ideas and attitudes of the generation of the 1960s. The socio-economic and ideological relations generating a group dissatisfied with an economically secure but diminishing horizon have been explicated often enough.[14] But it would be wrong to see the specificity of the New Left solely through these connections: The political mediation is also essential. We have to see critical and praxis theory as fitting into the ideological constraints and openings determined by a politics long dominated by Cold War anti-communism.

It is correct to see existentialists and beats as precursors of the New Left. Right-wing existentialism emerged out of a sense of despair among certain bourgeois intellectuals, to what they saw as the impossibility of social solutions to human problems. Even Left existentialism grew in an ideologically inbred atmosphere of doubts not only about capitalist but also socialist solutions, with Sartre's own version maintaining a constantly problematic relation with communism in the fifties, even as Sartre began to veer toward a New Left "Marxification" of his theories.[15] The beat movement was an early crystallization of hostility to the supposedly one-dimensional consumer society and to the authoritarian, bureaucratic and organizational constraints of advanced capitalism, but this hostility and cynicism were also directed toward any organized Left.

Stirred by seeing the limits of individualist solutions, collective foment at home and in the Third World, a group conditioned by existential and beat culture begins to crystallize as the New Left. The early stages of this formation are clearly marked by anti-communist, anti-Marxist and elitist feelings. But as they began to see that moral indignation and surrealist-style anarchism would not suffice, as they began to see the economic basis for the racism, foreign intervention and repression they struggled against, many New Leftists veered toward Marxism, first toward Trotskyism and then toward the Yugoslav-style socialism. The sources of these veerings should be clear: One might become a Marxist, but only if that Marxism was anti-Soviet.

As a growing movement the New Left is galvanized by the Cuban Revolution: Sartre and C. Wright Mills serve as the perfect bridges, the bearded Cuban revolutionaries are the perfect romantic symbols for the partial political awakening of a middle-class generation steeped in anti-establishment philosophy and poetry. Even after awakened anti-colonial and anti-racist feelings expand and extend to Vietnam, even as it becomes clear that the communist movement is the only powerful ally in these struggles, the New Left persists in its anti-communist posture. Here is a tremendous irony: that even long after Khruschev's so-called secret speech of 1956, the communist movement was completely identified with "Stalinism," and only anti-Soviet leftism served as the ideology for actions that would ultimately help liberation struggles mainly supported by the Soviet Union and Vietnamese communists.

This is not to deny the contribution of "old leftists" to the U.S. anti-war movement, but their field of action was limited in the wake of McCarthyism. Thus, to imagine a mass pro-communist left in the United States of the 1960s, and to criticize the New Left for its anti-communism or anarchism in the post-Cold War context of the United States is to miss the force of capitalism on political ideology.

Anti-communism creates the gap filled by Marcuse's critical theory and Sartre's existentialism; it accounts for the turn toward Fanon and Debray as theorists extending the New Left critique to the Third World and ethnic minorities in the advanced countries. The '60s marks the emergence of a growing educated sector (the largest ever to appear under capitalism), its ranks swollen by the post-war birth rates and economic boom, its thought radicalized by transformations and contradictions at home, exacerbated by the context of imperialist war. Their horizons blurred or blocked by a deadening consumerism, many young students desperately sought to play the central historical role they had been led to expect and saw all but lost in the increasingly managed and technologized organizations of advanced capitalism. They attempted to project themselves as the revolutionary "subject of history"; and when recognizing they were not numerous or strong enough for this, they turned to the ethnic minorities and third world groups in whose names they had already directed a considerable part of their revolt.

It was in the cauldron of this group's emerging weaknesses — the breast-beating and show-boating, the incipient disorganization and anarchism of a group in part fostered by its revolt against organization — that factions of the New Left, spurred on by Cuba and Vietnam, looked toward the heroes of guerrilla revolution — ironically to such creations of International Communist organizations as Ho Chi Minh and Mao Tse-Tung.

In the face of massive Soviet aid to Vietnam, it was to Mao's supposedly "anti-Stalinist" model of revolutionary struggle that the Marxist-inclined activists of the New Left turned. Only a left bred on anti-communism, a left open to aspects of Trotskyism and Frankfurt School criticism could have finally veered toward Maoism — if only because Maoism supposedly combined permanent and cultural revolution in a form said to involve praxis and constant attacks on bureaucracy. And it is no accident, either, that those New Leftists seeing the need finally for revolutionary party organization and discipline should turn on the anti-Soviet, anti-CP Mao of recent years, and that a fraction of these New Leftists should go so far in their bizarre historical transformation to finally re-read Stalin through Maoist eyes and take him on as image of revolutionary truth in opposition to the post-1956 "revisionism" of the Communist movement.

Thus the most rigid and sectarian notions of party organization are foisted under the banner of Fanshen-style workers' control and populism. A group glutted, alienated and "marginalized" by technologization of material production romanticizes an apology for lack of industrialization and identifies with a peasant culture which can never be its own.[16]

4. Some Conclusions

What are we to make of these developments? The New Left seems dead as a mass movement, many of its adherents now "integrated" or cultivating their private stereo-walled pot gardens. But New Left ideology lives on and is now reinforced by the continued publication of basic texts and critiques. Even some New Left spokesmen see the dissemination of New Left ideas as serving a regressive function at this juncture, since they point to capitalist evils, but fail to generate any real grasp of how to change them.

Nevertheless, New Left theorists are the radicals who most succeed in completing their studies and entering the universities where they now teach and publish New Left texts, and generate a new Left subculture, capturing the minds of many students who might be led in other directions. Thus our view that there is no way to simply negate the New Left, to mock or belittle it; one must be able to understand and transcend New Left concepts, taking their most positive aspects and placing them in a more satisfactory framework.

We must stand against both the right and the many left groups whose divisive strategies merely serve capitalism; we must stand for a coalition which, along with working class and other progressive elements, may include the most reasonable heirs to New Left theory. But to have an ideological means of passage, we must have a better grasp of the role of the New Left and the value and creativity of even exaggerated ideas which emerge outside given historical and party paradigms. Anarchism and utopianism cannot win revolutions, but liberation struggles and honest opposition to capitalism may be the seedbed for ideas which revitalize mass revolutionary movements. Lenin opposed the Second International to forge a strategy which spelled victory for the Russian masses. Fidel led a revolutionary struggle outside party parameters, though communists and workers had laid the groundwork, and though the Communist movement has been the only instrument able to resist imperialist counterattacks and to channel revolutionary energies toward the modulated construction of a new society and the new man New Leftists love to evoke. The future of France and Italy may turn out to be in Marxist hands, but this is in part due to the convergence of Communist Party and New Left influences on the minds of various discontented sectors of society.

Some may take a negative view of recent New and Old Left rapprochements; they may see a distortion of Marxism in recent European events. But, even in this country, New Left theories may in fact constitute a stage toward a total perspective that is very different from what their formulators originally intended. While negativities and dangers must be understood, the location and critical appropriation of New Left positivities may be vital to future historical developments.[17]

NOTES

1. Lenin, *Collected Works* (Moscow: Progress Publishers, 1974), 31: 17-117.
2. See Rosa Luxemburg, "Stagnation and Progress of Marxism," in *Karl Marx: A Symposium*, ed. D. Ryazanoff (London, 1929), pp. 105-14. There is renewed interest in Luxemburg among French Communists — cf. the recent publication of Gilbert Badia's *Rosa Luxemburg, Journalist, Polémiste, Révolutionnaire* (Paris: Editions Sociales, 1975).
3. Paul Piccone, "From Tragedy to Farce: The Return of Critical Theory," in *New German Critique*, 7 (Winter, 1976), pp. 91-104. Our discussion of the Hegelian Marxists (through page 32) is largely a critical summary of Piccone.
4. On Second International "crisis theory," see Andrew Arato, "Reexamining the Second International," in *Telos*, 18 (Winter, 1973-74), pp. 2-52.
5. Piccone, pp. 94-96.
6. *Ibid.*, pp. 96-97.
7. On the anti-Communist appropriation of the 1844 Manuscripts and its effect on the Communists who had first translated and propagated them in France, see Mark Poster, *Existential Marxism in Postwar France: From Sartre to Althusser* (Princeton: Princeton University Press, 1975), pp. 49-71, especially pp. 68-69.

8. See "Orthodox Marxism," in *History and Class Consciousness*, trans. Rodney Livingstone (Cambridge, Mass.: M.I.T. Press, 1971), pp. 1-27. Lenin's *Materialism and Empirio-Criticism* is the butt of constant New Left attacks — cf. John Hoffman, *Marxism and the Theory of Praxis* (New York: International Publishers, 1975), pp. 71-108. Lukács attacks Lenin only implicitly, while praising his dialectical politics — cf. Lukács' book of 1924, *Lenin: A Study of the Unity of His Thought* (Cambridge, Mass.: M.I.T. Press, 1971) and his article of 1970, "Lenin — Theoretician of Practice," in Georg Lukács, *Marxism and Human Liberation*, ed. E. San Juan, Jr. (New York: Dell, 1973), pp. 97-105.
9. Cf. Lukács' *Writer and Critic and Other Essays* (London: Merlin Press, 1970).
10. Cf. Lukacs' *Realism in Our Time* (New York: Harper and Row, 1964).
11. See Poster, *op. cit.*, pp. 36-37. Hoffman (*op. cit.*, p. 77) points to the *Textbook of Marxist Philosophy* (Gollancz, n.d.), prepared during the 1930s by the Leningrad Institute of Philosophy under M. Shirokov "for all Soviet institutions of higher education."
12. Piccone, pp. 97-98.
13. On the conjuncture of Frankfurt School negativity and Sartrean praxis philosophy (through the partial mediation of Yugoslav and Czech theorists), see Poster; also Eduard Batalov, *The Philosophy of Revolt* (Moscow: Progress Publishers, 1975).
14. Batalov's view, as set forth in the book review by Ileana Rodríguez, may be compared with that of "New Working Class" New Leftist, Alain Touraine, as reported by Eric Hobsbawm, in *Revolutionaries* (New York: Meridian, 1973), pp. 234-44.
15. Compare Sartre's *The Communists and the Peace*, trans. M. Fletcher and P. Beak (New York, 1968), and his later *Search for a Method*. For an account of Sartre's political-theoretical development, see Poster; also, H. Stuart Hughes, *The Obstructed Path* (New York: Harper and Row, 1966), pp. 153-226.
16. For a New Left attempt to explain this "obstructing path," see Paul Breines, "From Guru to Spectre: Marcuse and the Implosion of the Movement," in *Critical Interruptions* (New York: Herder and Herder, 1970).
17. On New Left anarchism, see Gil Green,*The New Radicalism: Anarchist or Marxist?* (New York: International Publishers, 1971). On New Left "Third World" theories, see Jack Woddis, *New Theories of Revolution* (New York: International Publishers, 1972). For the view that "the antagonism between an 'old' and a 'New' Left might be superseded," see Fredric Jameson, "Introduction/Prospectus: To Reconsider the Relationship of Marxism to Utopian Thought," in *Minnesota Review*, 6 (Spring, 1976), p. 55.

DISCUSSION [Simbolov and Rodríguez]

Question from the floor: When the term *petty bourgeois* arose, there really existed a large class of small property owners and the intelligentsia reflected the interests of this class. Today the numerical relationship has reversed. What then is the base of the intelligentsia today?

Reply by Rodríguez: It seems to me that there is a contradiction in Batalov. On the one hand he sees the intelligentsia as a class in transition: no longer a petty-bourgeois intelligentsia, but not yet a proletariat — rather right in between. But on the other hand, when he refers to the petty bourgeoisie, he is referring not mainly to the small property owners, but to the intelligentsia. Who are we after all? In a Marxist approach, class is determined by the relationship to the means of production, to the production of commodities and surplus values. What is the particular commodity that we as intellectuals produce? We see a tendency toward proletarianization. I think that Batalov is correct in saying that we are going in that direction, but the term *lumpen bourgeoisie* does not seem to fit.

Reply by Simbolov: An attempt is being made to find a word to express the changed relationship of a large number of people, such as those who today are in the universities. People do not like the term "new working class," because it suggests that in fact they are a congealed class rather than something that is in a process of transition. But even if the intellectuals are in the process of being proletarianized they still carry intellectual traditions which stem from the time when the terminology arose. I do not find a disagreement in terms of what is happening, but in expressing what is happening without each time giving a two-hour explanation. It does seem to me, however, that there is a traditional petty-bourgeois baggage which clings to a group in the process of transformation, even as it takes on new relations.

Comment from the floor: It seems to me that the characterization of the New Left by the previous speakers as anti-Soviet is a kind of McCarthyism in reverse. It is only in those countries like France and Italy, where the Communist Parties have created a great distance between themselves and the Soviet Union, that the Communist Parties have a great deal of influence. A lot of people in this country feel that the relationship between the Communist Party and Moscow is much too close and that the forms of politics in the Soviet Union would be a regression in this country.

Reply by Simbolov: I did not mean my paper to be an analysis of what it means to be anti-Soviet. That would have taken a different paper. What I tried to stress was my own sense of priorities. The New Left has tendencies to use the word "process" and to stress the need to see things as an historical process. But there is not much of an analysis of process to be found in the New Left in terms of the situation in the Soviet Union. We have criticism of the Soviet Union from every different side, criticism that they are not democratic enough, criticism that they are not Stalinist or radical enough. We find that after 1968, when the New Left essentially starts to leave Marcuse behind, they went in these two different directions.

Comment from the floor: Despite the fact that the Communist Parties of Italy and France want to go on their own national paths, the New Left there splits from the Communist Parties, so that it is not only anti-Soviet, but anti-Communist Party as a party. One can say there is a general tendency in the New Left which is against the organized mass parties. There was a reaction earlier against the "fathers" of the New Left, Adorno and the others (but not so much Marcuse) for not doing anything, and this led to new organizational forms in the New Left.

Reply by Simbolov: But if you looked at the situation you would find that they went in every direction except into the Communist Party. That is what happened in fact in 1968, '69, and '70. Now, certain of those sectors are turning back to the Communist Party.

Comment from the floor: It is worth remembering that the Communist Parties of Italy and France were the biggest Communist Parties in the West even at the height of the period when it was fashionable to call them "Soviet dominated." Now the anti-Communist press makes any differences among Communist Parties appear to be far greater than they actually are. The Berlin Conference of 29 European Communist Parties in fact showed general agreement on all questions dealing with imperialism, detente, and the need for building coalitions with Socialists and non-proletarian forces in the capitalist countries of Europe. In the United States, the Communist Party subscribes to the principle long held by the Communist movement and reaffirmed at the Berlin conference that each Party must develop specific forms of political struggle based on the specific characteristics of the situation in the country.

MARXISM, REVISIONISM, AND THE STATE

Terence Ball
University of Minnesota

1

Paraphrasing an aphorism of Hegel's, Marx once remarked that history does indeed repeat itself — "the first time as tragedy, the second as farce."[1] The observation applies no less aptly to controversies within the history of Marxian theory and practice itself. The Marxian analysis of the state is a case in point. Early in this century the Revisionists — Bernstein and Kautsky foremost among them — attempted to make Marxism "respectable" by de-emphasizing its revolutionary content. Socialist society, on their view, could, as the title of Bernstein's best-known book suggests, "evolve" piecemeal and pacifically from bourgeois society.[2] And since the brougeois state (or "civil society," in the Hegelian phrase sometimes preferred by Marx) was to "wither away," there would then be no need for an interim "dictatorship of the proletariat."[3] This "doctoring of Marxism" was subjected to a telling critique by Lenin in *The State and Revolution*.[4] That was not, however, the end of the matter.

Indeed, today history repeats itself. If the bowdlerizing of Marx by the Revisionists was a tragedy, the current "rediscovery" of a respectable / young / Hegelian / humanist / social democratic Marx has all the makings of a farce. The *farceurs* include those whose brand of Marxism has affinities with religion of one kind

(Christianity)[5] or another (Zen Buddhism);[6] with a contentless "humanism";[7] with philosophical idealism;[8] with piecemeal reformism and social democracy;[9] and so on. If these reformulations and reinterpretations of Marxian theory were idle tea-time amusements, one might not object. Matters are not, alas, so simple as that. For theoretical speculation has a way of spilling over into political practice. And this tendency is nowhere more evident than in some current "Marxian" analyses which view the state as a reconciler of class interests and reject as outmoded the concept of proletarian dictatorship.

Needless to say, these views bear a closer examination than can be provided here. But if we cannot resolve all the problems associated with the Marxian analylsis of the state, we may nevertheless be able to clarify some of the more important ones. It should at any rate be possible to expose and clear up some persistent misrepresentations of Marx's own position.

2

Marx's analysis of the state may be divided into two parts. On the one hand both he and Engels sketched the history, the structure, and the supporting ideology of the bourgeois state, and, on the other, of the transitional state or quasi-state which Marx called the dictatorship of the proletariat. Marx's critics complain that Marx had little to say about the former, and even less about the latter. Thus, for example, Lichtheim: "Leaving aside Marx's sketchy observations on the . . . Paris Commune, and his quasi-Jacobin reference to 'proletarian dictatorship' during the transition period, his followers were left without guidance."[11] Yet Marx's "oversight" was — so his critics maintain — understandable and even justifiable in the light of two considerations. Marx neglected the bourgeois state in the first place because he viewed all political institutions as *epiphenomenal*, that is, as mere froth upon the deep ocean of economic currents.[12] Moreover, Marx viewed the state as being unworthy of study in its own right, inasmuch as it was a transitory institution which would shortly "wither away."[13]

In fact, neither of these claims is true; nor, for that matter, is it true that Marx almost entirely neglected the bourgeois state. Marx actually had quite a lot to say about the state (or "civil society"), beginning with his *Critique of Hegel's Philosophy of Right* in 1843, his essay on the Jewish Question in 1844, *The German Ideology* in 1847, *The Communist Manifesto* in 1848, *The Eighteenth Brumaire* in 1852, his *Critique of the Gotha Program* in 1875, and *The Civil War in France* in 1871; and likewise Engels in *Anti-Dühring* in 1878 and *The Origin of the Family, Private Property and the State* in 1884. Still, it is true that Marx himself wrote no sustained and systematic treatise on the state. Yet that does not mean that he thought the subject unimportant. On the contrary, Marx went so far as to draft a plan for a "Work on the Modern State."[14] Why he never carried out this plan must remain a matter of speculation.

Although necessarily somewhat speculative, two explanations suggest themselves. First of all, Marx's apparent preoccupation with economic factors rather than political ones — with "base" rather than "superstructure" — was no doubt due in part to his struggle against utopian moralizers and idealists within the European socialist movement itself. Moreover, many of their mistaken claims derived from mistaken economic doctrines (*vide* Proudhon). If Weitling, Lassalle, and others emphasized the importance of moral-political factors, Marx was all the more determined to emphasize material and economic factors. Slogans, as Marx was fond of saying, are no substitute for science. Yet Marx's adversaries within the socialist movement offered little more than slogans, and "humanist" ones at that — peace, justice, and brotherly love. Annenkov recalls a heated exchange between Marx and Weitling. "The raising of fantastic hopes," Marx argued, could lead "only to the final ruin and not to the saving of the sufferers. To call to the workers without any strictly scientific ideas or constructive doctrines . . . was equivalent to vain and dishonest play at preaching which assumed on the one hand an inspired prophet and on the other only gaping asses."[15] A similar criticism of Lassalle is to be found in the *Critique of the Gotha Program*.

In any event it seems safe to say that Marx's reputation as an economic determinist is due to the struggle he waged against his utopian adversaries within the socialist movement: If they emphasized moral and political factors, Marx countered by stressing the importance of economic and material factors. In retrospect it appears that Marx went too far in that direction. Indeed, Engels later admitted as much:

> Marx and I are ourselves partly to blame for the fact that the younger people sometimes lay more stress on the economic side than is due to it. We had to emphasize the main principle vis-a-vis our adversaries, who denied it, and we had not always the time, the place, or the opportunity to give their due to the other elements involved in the interaction.[16]

In short: Marx's apparent "failure" to emphasize political factors — the state, most notably — itself has a *political* explanation.

Even so, two quite misleading claims are still given credence in some circles. The first is that the state, as a political institution, is "epiphenomenal" vis-a-vis more fundamental economic factors; or — to put it another way — the form and content of the state-as-superstructure is uniquely determined by the economy-as-base. Thus the state itself is unworthy of sustained and systematic study. Hence Marx's "neglect" of the state. In fact, however, it was not Marx who neglected the state, but some latter-day "Marxists" who neglected Marx. The Second International paid little attention to the capitalist state *as such*, and much to the economic "base." As Poulantzas explains,

> The absence of a study of the state derived from the fact that the dominant conception of [the Second International] was a deviation, *economism*, which is generally accompanied by an absence of revolutionary strategies and objectives . . . . In effect, economism considers that the other levels of social reality, including the state, are simple epiphenomena reducible to the economic "base." Thereby a specific study of the State becomes superfluous. Parallel with this, economism considers that every change in the social system happens first of all in the economy and that political action should have the economy as its principal objective. Once again, a specific study of the state is redundant. Thus economism leads either to reformism and trade-unionism, or to forms of "leftism" such as syndicalism.[17]

Despite his reputation as an economic determinist, Marx repeatedly stressed the importance of distinctively *political* strategies and objectives. This can be seen not only in his writings — the *Eighteenth Brumaire* and *The Civil War in France*, for example — but in his life. As Engels remarked, Marx was before all else a *revolutionary*.[18] And it is this revolutionary, i.e., *political*, element that runs like a red thread (pun intended) through all Marx's works. This is true even, as Engels remarked, of *Capital* — supposedly the fullest, most systematic defense of "economic determinism."[19] Thus, for example, in the chapter on the working day Marx emphasizes the importance of legislation as it affects the hours and working conditions of the proletariat.[20] And in the section on "primitive accumulation," Marx emphasizes the political and legislative means employed by the rising bourgeoisie to attain, and subsequently to consolidate and legitimize, their economic dominance.[21]

No doubt many other instances of Marx's specifically *political* interests and acumen could be trotted out; but it may suffice to remark that, contrary to a popular stereotype, Marx was not a strict economic determinist for whom a political analysis of the state was superfluous. Far from being a "political primitive" who "could not develop a political science or a political theory because he had no recognition of politics as an autonomous field of activity,"[22] Marx was prescient in his analyses of political affairs. If he paid less attention to distinctively "political" matters than, say, Lenin, that is because Marx was dealing with different adversaries. Marx's and Lenin's *conjunctures* (to borrow a favorite term of Althusser's) were quite different, and so it is hardly surprising that Marx appears in retrospect to have been an economic determinist and Lenin a political activist.[23] The point to remember is that their respective emphases are to be explained *politically*, that is, by reference to the internal politics of the socialist movement.

3

I have so far suggested two things. The first is that the degree to which Marx neglected to study the state has been much exaggerated by his critics; the second, that Marx's having paid relatively more attention to "economic" than to "political" factors is traceable not to his having been an "economic determinist" but to the internal politics of the socialist movement itself. Two further claims remain to be considered. The first is that Marx neglected the bourgeois state because he believed it to be a *transitory* phenomenon (or, in the economic determinist version of that claim, a transitory *epiphenomenon*). The second claim to be considered is that Marx expected the bourgeois state to "wither away." The first claim is, at best, half true; the second is utterly false. Let us see why.

As to the first claim: Certainly Marx believed the bourgeois state to be a transitory phenomenon. It had not always existed, nor would it last forever.[24] That much, at least, is true. But it is a *non sequitur* to say that *because* Marx believed the bourgeois state to be a transitory phenomenon, he *therefore* thought it unworthy of systematic study. That the latter is not entailed by the former may be easily demonstrated. For consider: Marx also believed the capitalist mode of production to be a passing or transitory phenomenon; yet he devoted his adult life to studying its natural history, its inner workings, and its emerging contradictions. Enough said about a manifestly silly argument.

The remaining claim — that Marx expected the bourgeois state to pass peacefully away of its own accord — is quite evidently false. But, more importantly, it serves as a premise in an equally fallacious argument. This argument runs as follows: The bourgeois state loses its bourgeois or dominant-class character when the franchise is extended to the working class; the bourgeois state as such will then disappear; hence there is *no need* for (1) a revolutionary seizing of power by the proletariat, and, subsequently, for (2) a revolutionary dictatorship of the proletariat. Let us consider first the false premise, and then go on to criticize the "evolutionist" argument which rests upon it.

The claim that the bourgeois state will wither away is false in two senses. It is first of all *factually* false, inasmuch as it misrepresents Marx's and Engels' views on the matter. It is not the bourgeois state that will wither away, but the transitional proletarian state. As for the bourgeois state, Marx and Engels speak repeatedly of the necessity of *abolishing* it. The revisionist (or "evolutionist") claim is false in a second, *theoretical* sense. For, according to Marxian theory, the state exists precisely in order to protect the interests of the dominant class; the very existence of a state apparatus — police, courts, prisons, army, etc. — attests to the existence of classes in society, and, moreover, to the domination of one class by another. (This is true no matter which class is dominant; that is, it is true not only of the bourgeois state but of the proletarian state as well.) Such domination is all the more pervasive and stable when it appears to be legitimate, even in the eyes of the subordinate class. To maintain appearances is after all the function of the legitimating state apparatus — "free" elections, "impartial" courts of law, etc. To suppose that these agencies as presently constituted even *could* be the instruments of significant social transformation (e.g., socializing the means of production, eliminating class distinctions, etc.) is to confuse their function and to accept the prevailing ideology.

A characteristic mistake of the revisionists was their conflation of a crucial distinction, viz., the distinction between holding state *office* and having state *power*. The two are by no means equivalent. A working class party may well gain state office without thereby acquiring state power. But to have the former without the latter is to have the form without the substance, that is to say, the *symbol* of power without the reality. * The fate of the Allende regime in Chile is the most recent reminder of the tragic consequences awaiting working class parties which forget the lessons of history and theory.

NOTES

Abbreviations of works cited:
- *LSW:* Lenin, *Selected Works* in one volume (Moscow: Progress Publishers, 1968)
- *MECW:* Marx and Engels, *Collected Works* (Moscow, London and New York: International, 1975-)
- *MESW:* Marx and Engels, *Selected Works* in one volume (New York: International, 1968)

1. Marx, "The Eighteenth Brumaire of Louis Bonaparte," *MESW*, p. 97.

2. Eduard Bernstein, *Evolutionary Socialism* (New York: Schocken 1909).
3. Karl Kautsky, *Dictatorship of the Proletariat* (Ann Arbor: University of Michigan Press, 1964).
4. *LSW*, p. 265.
5. See, e.g., Giulio Girardi, *Marxism and Christianity* (New York: MacMillan, 1968); and Roger Garaudy, *From Anathema to Dialogue* (London: Collins, 1967).
6. See Fromm in D.T. Suzuki, Erich Fromm, and Richard DeMartino, *Zen Buddhism and Psychoanalysis* (New York: Harper, 1960), and elsewhere.
7. See, e.g., Erich Fromm, ed., *Socialist Humanism* (New York: Anchor Books, 1966).
8. E.g., Shlomo Avineri, *The Social and Political Thought of Karl Marx* (Cambridge: Cambridge University Press, 1968).
9. E.g., George Lichtheim, *Marxism: An Historical and Critical Study* (New York: Praeger, 1963).
10. See, *inter alia*, Mihailo Marković, *The Contemporary Marx: Essays on Humanist Communism* (Nottingham: Spokesman Books, 1974); and *From Affluence to Praxis* (Ann Arbor: University of Michigan Press, 1974); Gajo Petrović, *Marx in the Mid-Twentieth Century* (Garden City, New York: Anchor Books, 1967); Svetozar Stojanović, *Between Ideals and Reality* (New York: Oxford University Press, 1973); and generally, the recently suppressed journal *Praxis*. Cf. also the programs of the French and Italian Communist Parties — and in particular M. Marchais' Report to the 22nd Congress of the French C.P., 4 February 1976.
11. Lichtheim, *op. cit.*, p. 372.
12. *Ibid.*, pp. 373, 375.
13. *Ibid.*, p. 373.
14. *MECW*, IV, p. 666.
15. Quoted in David McLellan, *Karl Marx* (London: Macmillan, 1973), pp. 156-57.
16. Engels to Bloch, *MESW*, p. 693.
17. Nicos Poulantzas, "The Problem of the Capitalist State," *New Left Review*, 58 (Nov.-Dec. 1969), pp. 67-78, at 68.
18. Engels, "Speech at the Graveside of Karl Marx," *MESW*, p. 436.
19. Engels to Mehring, *MESW*, p. 699.
20. Marx, *Capital*, I (New York: International, 1967), ch. X.
21. *Ibid.*, Part VIII, *passim*.
22. Samuel P. Huntington, *Political Order in Changing Societies* (New Haven, Conn.: Yale University Press, 1969), p. 336.
23. *Loc. cit.*
24. The fullest elaboration and defense of this view is to be found in Engels' *Origin of the Family, Private Property and the State*, in *MESW*, p. 537f.

DISCUSSION

Comment from the floor: I think there is a serious problem as regards dictatorship of the proletariat. The first time the French Communist Party mentioned it since 1925 was when they said that they did not believe in it any more, hardly having used it even in programmatic ways. As far as I know, the Italian Communist Party still endorses the concept as an ultimate goal, beyond a coalition government with the Christian Democrats.

Reply: You can't discard that as so much excess baggage; it goes to the very heart of class analysis that is provided by Marxian theory.

Comment from the floor: I think we have to be a little careful in making a leap from the question of taking office to taking power. I don't believe, for example, that it is correct to think that the Chile experience proves that you cannot take power by democratic means. You could say that Allende never did take power — he took office. The problem was to find a means of passage from office to power. Chile does not have the same kind of industrial development as France; they do not have many of the things which would enable a Communist-Socialist group to move from the point of taking office to where they would have power.

Comment from the floor: I think that in Italy and France it is important to have a deep understanding of how the class struggles work in those countries. You can abolish the term dictatorship of the proletariat without abolishing the concept. In the northern sector of Italy and the industrial sector of France, a good part of the working class has already developed a consciousness. The problem is to convince the middle class that their interests lie with the working class.

Comment from the floor: We have a problem of keeping the term dictatorship, or at least keeping the concept, so that it can be made clear that the state is a dictatorship. This is a form of knowledge about the state. In every socialist revolution in this century there have been coalitions with other parties and with other sectors. It has never been the proletariat by itself that has done this. The problem is not to be ignorant about the nature of the state.

Comment from the floor: As was pointed out, the concept dictatorship really refers to the content of the state rather than its form. It does not depend on the ability of those who are in control of the state to understand the nature of it. This was very apparent in Eastern Europe after World War II, when the form of people's democracy was regarded as an alternative to dictatorship of the proletariat, and it was not until later that it was realized that it actually was a form of the dictatorship of the proletariat. During the Civil War in the United States we had to free the slaves by presidential decree. There was no way, according to the Constitution, to deprive the slaveowners of their property by presidential decree. It was an exercising of the option of arbitrary rule by a class, an expression of the dictatorship of the bourgeoisie, but without the ideologists of capitalism understanding the true content of the state. I think the same situation may develop, say in France or Italy, in the sense that if there is a transition to power by a Socialist-Communist coalition, the subsequent development of a dictatorship of the proletariat may not take place consciously. It will be done as: "Let us introduce changes to meet our problems." After all, socialism has not reached a single country under the slogan of socialism. Every country that has adopted a socialist form did so on the basis of meeting very fundamental needs like "peace, bread, and land," etc. The transition that generally took place was a transition from a dictatorship of workers and peasants into a dictatorship of the proletariat after the country had been freed from the control of monopoly capital or imperialism. Such a transition is necessary because the peasantry will not initiate the transformation of their property from private property to property of the people as a whole. This initiative can come only from the working class. The class nature of the state as a dictatorship of the proletariat is determined when the working class actually controls or dominates the process of further social transformation.

Comment from the floor: Although I agree very much with the concept of dictatorship here, the use of the term can be very damaging in many situations. The U.S. Communist Party has not been using the term "dictatorship of the proletariat" since the 1930s. Instead, they talk about how the Senate is 90 percent corporate lawyers and how things would be if instead it were 90 percent workers. But they do not come out like a trumpet, "Da-ta-da, we are no longer using the term."

SCIENCE AS A SCIENCE

Erwin Marquit
University of Minnesota

In an essay on Engels' *Socialism: Utopian and Scientific* (hereafter *SUS*), Darko Suvin[1] undertakes a wide-ranging critical analysis of this Marxist classic and concludes that the connotations of the two terms, *utopian* and *scientific*, "have changed so much that Engels' main meanings are indeed no more immediately usable" and that the basic opposition embodied in the title has become misleading and even counterproductive.

A close examination of Suvin's essay, however, discloses that Suvin's criticisms deal not so much with the change in connotations of Engels' terms as with the underlying content of the work itself, as Engels meant it to be understood. Moreover, Suvin's criticisms themselves cannot stand up to critical analysis.

Suvin's analysis is divided into three sections. The present analysis will be similarly structured to correspond to Suvin's sections. The discussion which follows does not pretend to be an exhaustive analysis of all of Suvin's misreadings of Marx and Engels, but only deals with the key points in Suvin's criticisms.

1

Suvin identifies what he sees as two opposed clusters emerging from Parts 1 and 2 of *SUS*, which he tabulates in what he says are Engels' own terms as follows:

Idealistic and utopian	*Materialistic and scientific*
head—thinking—principles	reality — facts and deeds —
reason — from outside the society	real things and processes— [from within the society]
absolute truth	historical view

Suvin calls this a black-or-white, exclusive model, which cannot be taken seriously. "Marx," wrote Suvin, "was surely building a system pretending to a fairly absolute or near-perfect truth, surely he thought with his head, applied reason, had principles, lived on the margins of society, and so on." Suvin argues that what matters "is not the fact that the 'utopian' socialists built a system from their head: Marx did so too. But he, as different from them, NOT ONLY used reason, his head, principles, etc., BUT ALSO took into account reality, facts, and historico-economical processes — all of which culminated in his discovery of the theory of surplus value which revealed the innermost secret of capitalist production."

It is true that Engels juxtaposed an approach to socialism that is idealistic and utopian to one that is materialistic and scientific. But it is simply not true that Engels identified the terms *idealistic* and *utopian* with the terms under that heading on the left side of Suvin's table, nor did Engels identify the terms *materialistic* and *scientific* with the terms under that heading on the right side of Suvin's table. Suvin thus combats a straw man that is not to be found in *SUS*. Let us look at some of the main points made by Engels and summarize them to see what comparisons Engels actually made.

In discussing the French, English and German utopians, Engels wrote that to them

> socialism is the expression of absolute truth, reason and justice, and has only to be discovered to conquer all the world by virtue of its own power. And as absolute truth is independent of time, space, and of the historical development of man, it is a mere accident when and where it is discovered. With all this, absolute truth, reason, and justice are different with the founder of

> each different school. And as each one's special kind of absolute truth, reason, and justice is again conditioned by his subjective understanding, his conditions of existence, the measure of his knowledge and his intellectual training, there is no other ending possible in this conflict of absolute truths than they shall be mutually exclusive one of the other. Hence, from this nothing could come but a kind of eclectic, average socialism, which, as a matter of fact, has up to the present time dominated the minds of most of the socialist workers in France and England. Hence, a mish-mash allowing of the most manifold shades of opinion; a mish-mash of such critical statements, economic theories, pictures of future society by the founders of different sects, as excite a minimum of opposition; a mish-mash which is the more easily brewed the more the definite sharp edges of the individual constituents are rubbed down in the stream of debate, like rounded pebbles in a brook.[2] (p. 126)

Thus, according to Engels, the utopians were idealistic and unscientific not because they used their heads to think, but because their thoughts were based on notions associated with philosophical idealism, that is, concepts such as absolute truth, reason and justice independent of space, time and historical development of man. Moreover, such concepts undergo no change because they are appropriate to all conditions of human existence. Hence they are not only idealistic, but also, as Engels indicated in Part 2 of *SUS*, nondialectical, that is mechanistic (metaphysical). With this static nonmaterialistic conception of society the early (utopian) socialism could only criticize the existing capitalistic mode of production and its consequences. But, as Engels wrote:

> it could not explain them, and, therefore, could not get the mastery of them. It could only simply reject them as bad. The more strongly this earlier socialism denounced the exploitation of the working class, inevitable under capitalism, the less able was it clearly to show in what this exploitation consisted and how it arose. But for

> this it was necessary — (1) to present the capitalistic method of production in its historical connection and its inevitableness during a particular historical period, and therefore, also, to present its inevitable downfall; and (2) to lay bare its essential character, which was still a secret. This was done by the discovery of *surplus value*. It was shown that the appropriation of unpaid labor is the basis of the capitalist mode of production and of the exploitation of the worker that occurs under it. (p. 133)

In the next paragraph Engels referred to point (1) above as the *materialistic conception of history* and not as *historical view*, as suggested by Suvin in his table. There is an important difference. After all, Hegel also had an historical view and treated history as a dialectical process, but his treatment of history was not materialistic.

By the phrase "materialistic conception of history" Engels meant not only the materialist content of Marx's analysis, but also its dialectical content. In Part 2, Engels wrote:

> The perception of the fundamental contradiction in German idealism led necessarily back to materialism, but, *nota bene*, not to the simply metaphysical, exclusively mechanical materialism of the eighteenth century. Old materialism looked upon all previous history as a crude heap of irrationality and violence; modern materialism sees in it the process of evolution of humanity and aims at discovering the laws thereof. (p. 131)

Without this materialist conception of history the utopians were unable to see basic socio-economic changes as a process developing on the field of class struggle, and that a socialist society would emerge from this struggle. For them, the only path to socialism would be propaganda and model experiments.

From the foregoing discussion, it follows that Engels' contrasting of utopian socialism with scientific socialism does not at all correspond to Suvin's table. In fact, Engels' contrast should look as follows:

Utopian socialism	Scientific socialism
mechanistic idealist	dialectical materialist
society to correspond to absolute concepts of the ideal	society as a form of matter subject to laws of development
socialism to be attained through propaganda and model experiments	socialism to be a consequence of class struggle
no theory of social development	knowledge of laws of social development possible and necessary
class concepts absent	understanding of science of society requiring proletarian outlook

It is clear that the ideological positions here are irreconcilable. Moreover, Suvin presents not a shred of evidence to justify his attempt to separate the views of Engels from those of Marx. In fact, Engels attributes the discovery of the materialist conception of history to Marx. And Marx's writings are permeated with the content of scientific socialism indicated above. Suvin's table shows such a distorted view of Engels' work that it is little wonder that he "do[es] not see how Marx can be differentiated from the major 'utopian socialists'" by means of his table.

Before closing the discussion on the first section of Suvin's essay, we should take a look at Suvin's charge that Engels thought it necessary to combat the utopians "in the same way as — only harder than — full-fledged enemies." Suvin presents no evidence to support this charge. Although critical of the approach that would lead the socialist movement into a blind alley, Engels nowhere displays such fury against Saint-Simon, Fourier, and Owen. On the contrary, Engels wrote of Robert Owen: "Every social movement, every real advance in England on behalf of the workers links itself on to the name of Robert Owen." (p. 125)

2

The second section of Suvin's essay begins with a lengthy discussion of what he calls the "semantic context of 'science' in Engels' time and space," a discussion based largely on the work of the German lexicographers, Jakob and Wilhelm Grimm. In this way Suvin traces the German meaning of the word *science* from "knowledge, intelligence, notion, understanding" to "one of the two supreme goods of the German nation and indeed of mankind (the other being the much older *Kunst* or art)." And as regards this last meaning, Suvin adds: "There is no doubt that Engels too takes it [science] in this sense." It is difficult to imagine that Suvin really believes that this last contribution from him could shed any light on the question of the usefulness of *SUS*, but apparently he does.

In Marxism, the meaning of the term *science* is inseparably bound up with the Marxist theory of knowledge. To understand what the term meant to Engels one should not refer to lexicographic description, but to the state of the Marxist theory of knowledge at the time Engels wrote *SUS*. Likewise, any evaluation of the appropriateness of Engels' conception of science in the present period must be based on a comparison of the state of the Marxist theory of knowledge at the present time with that in Engels' time and not on shifts in the meaning of the term in bourgeois epistemology. Suvin makes no attempt to do this and therefore his lexicographic discussion is not so much harmless drudgery as it is sand in the reader's eyes, a discussion that adds nothing to an evaluation of the relevance of *SUS* today.

In the latter part of the second section, Suvin mounts his major attack on the concept of scientific socialism by asserting that there is a lack of parallelism in Engels' treatment of the sciences of history and nature. (For most purposes, the term *history* here can be replaced by the term *society*.) Marxism is, after all, a monistic world view. Engels pointed out that in the Hegelian system "for the first time the whole world, natural, historical, and intellectual" is represented as a dialectical process. It took the replacement of Hegelian idealism by materialsm to remove the fundamental contradiction of the Hegelian system — its claim, according to Engels, that "things and their evolution were only the realised pictures of the 'Idea' existing somewhere from eternity before the world was." The Hegelian system claimed to be the very essence of absolute truth, a system of natural and historical knowledge embracing everything and final for all time, in contradiction to the fundamental law of dialectical reasoning. (p. 130)

The science of history and the science of nature thus concern themselves with the laws of motion and development of two forms of the material world, society and nature, both subject to the same dialectical processes. If any part of this system breaks down, then dialectical materialism, as a monistic world view, collapses.

To demonstrate the lack of parallelism between Engels' science of nature and science of history Suvin again resorts to a table. The first three entries deal with the dialectical materialist content of both the science of nature and the science of history and the law-governed character of both. But the fourth entry in the science of history — "Must be representative of proletarian class interests, not 'absolute truth' etc." — has no parallel in the science-of-nature column, the blank space being filled by question marks.

"If this tabulation is correct," writes Suvin, "the careful parallel of Engels' contains nonetheless a glaring blind spot (marked by the question-marks above), which invalidates much of his reasoning. For *either* science too is finally an ideology, a 'superstructure' (Ueberbau) on the 'real . . . economic structure of society' . . . *or* . . . an approximation of absolute truth . . . and all the fulminations against the 'utopians' search after absolute truth, justice, etc., are unwarranted. . . . In the first case . . . science would be itself ideologically corrupted by class society. In the second case, utopianism . . . would not be wrong in principle."

Three fundamental errors in Suvin's analysis above are immediately evident.

The first error lies in the fourth entry under the science of history. Instead of "Must be representative of proletarian class interests, not 'absolute truth,' etc.," this entry should be "objectively existing society as the ultimate source of theoretical knowledge." Then the fourth entry under the science of nature would be, correspondingly, "objectively existing nature as the ultimate source of theoretical knowledge." In this way the gap vanishes. We will deal with the question of the theoretical content of scientific socialism in section 3.

Suvin's second error really represents a compound error. Here he demands his own "exclusive" model: EITHER science is an ideology OR it is an approximation of absolute truth, when in reality science can also be embraced by his "subsumptive" model: NOT ONLY can science be an ideology, BUT ALSO an approximation of absolute truth.

Suvin is disturbed that Engels criticized the utopians, Saint-Simon, Fourier and Owen, because "not one of them appears as a representative of the interests of that proletariat which historical development had, in the meantime, produced." (p. 117) Moreover, Engels also stated that scientific socialism is a reflection of the objectively existing conflict between the productive forces and the mode of production and that this theoretical knowledge was accessible, first of all, to the working class, namely the class which had a vital interest in the practical application of this knowledge to the objectively existing class struggle in order to improve the objective conditions of its existence.

If we consider the science of nature we find similarly that scientific theory is a reflection of objectively existing nature and support for such theoretical research comes first of all from that segment of society that stands to gain from application of the theory to nature. Theoretical knowledge of nature and society both have a social basis. There is nothing strange about the fact that the bourgeoisie, as a class, is interested in hindering the scientific study of a theory which will become an ideological weapon in the struggle to abolish the class division of society and with it also the bourgeoisie. We do not see, nor do we expect to see, cigarette companies making a serious effort to study the harmful effects of smoking. Individual members of the bourgeoisie may be able to cast aside their prejudices and come to understand the objective laws of scientific socialism, but the bourgeoisie as a class will use its resources to wage an ideological struggle against its own demise.

Unlike previous social transformations, the transition to socialism is not spontaneous, but takes place consciously. Since the working class has the historic mission of playing the leading role in such a transition, it has no interest in a corrupted or distorted view of the science of society, but on the contrary, it has a vital interest in the most accurate understanding of the science of society in order to make most effective use of this knowledge. The bourgeoisie, on the other hand, generates an ideological superstructure designed to maintain the exploitative class relations; it will not subsidize a science of society that could be used as a weapon to bring an end to such class relations.

Suvin's third error involves confusion of the term *absolute truth* as used in metaphysical reasoning with its use in the Marxist theory of knowledge. In Marxist theory, knowledge is both relative and absolute. It is relative, because at any given moment it is incomplete, partial, and, to a certain extent, limited by the social conditions in which it is acquired. It is also absolute, because insofar as it actually does reflect the objective reality, it has a certain true or absolute content. Suvin confuses absolute truth in this latter sense with the absolute truth, reason and justice sought by the utopian socialists without any connection of the historical process to the present objectively existing society. For example, the fact that there is no such thing as absolute space or time independent of matter does not mean that space and time have no objective existence as properties of matter. To the extent that these temporal and spatial properties are known, they constitute an approximation of absolute truth.

3

In the third section, Suvin directs his criticisms to the very heart of historical materialism.

He begins the discussion by asserting that historical materialism has not solved the problem of economic predetermination and ideologico-political free will.

Let us begin by citing Engels' discussion of the theoretical basis of scientific socialism:

> The new productive forces have already outgrown the capitalistic mode of using them. And this conflict between productive forces and modes of production is not a conflict engendered in the mind of man, like that between original sin and divine justice. It exists, in fact, objectively, outside us, independently of the will and actions even of the men that have brought it on. Modern socialism is nothing but the reflex, in thought, of this conflict in fact; its ideal reflection in the minds, first, of the class directly suffering under it, the working class. (p. 134)

Suvin says of this paragraph that it is the "extreme deterministic formulation of the essay. . . . This prevailing determinism leads on the one hand to a crassly mechanical materialism. . . . Complementarily . . . it leads to a historical optimism politically as unrealistic as that of the utopians."

What Suvin really objects to is the basic Marxist position that there exist objective laws of development of society. If such laws exist then the study of such laws becomes the science of society. Suvin arbitrarily says that any belief in the existence of such laws leads to mechanical materialism. But if this were so, why does belief in the existence of such objective laws of development of nature not also lead Marxists automatically to a mechanical rather than dialectical materialist approach to nature? The issue is really whether the conflict Engels speaks of is dependent on or independent of the will of man. The answer lies in the response to the question which Engels himself poses: "Now in what does this conflict consist?" In answering this question Engels goes into a description of Marx's economic analysis of capitalist production, and in doing so enumerates various conflicts or contradictions that arise as a consequence of the capitalist mode of production itself, independently of the will of the individual capitalists. First of all, there is the contradiction between the socialized nature of the labor process by which commodities are produced and the private appropriation by the capitalist of the product of this socialized labor.

> This contradiction, which gives to the new mode of production its capitalistic character, *contains the germ of the whole of the social antagonisms today.* (p. 137)

This contradiction is that between the socialized nature of the labor process by which the commodities are produced and the private appropriation by the capitalist of the product of this socialized labor. As Marx showed in *Capital*, this conflict is not consciously created by the capitalist. From his point of view he sees only the exchange of value for value, that is, the exchange of labor power for wages. But, as Engels notes:

> *The contradiction between socialized production and capitalistic appropriation manifested itself as the antagonism of proletariat and bourgeoisie.* (p. 138)

Further, Engels discusses Marx's theory of economic crises:

> Advantages in natural or artificial conditions of production now decide the existence or nonexistence of individual capitalists, as well as of whole industries and countries. He that falls is remorselessly cast aside. It is the Darwinian struggle of the individual for existence transferred from Nature to society with intensified violence. The conditions of existence natural to the animal appear as the final term of human development. The contradiction between soci-

> alised production and capitalistic appropriation now presents itself as *an antagonism between the organisation of production in the individual workshop and the anarchy of production in society generally.* (p. 140)

Here again we deal with a law of development of capitalism. Although the consciousness of individual capitalists or capitalist entities plays a role in the outcome of particular aspects of the struggle, the fact that the struggle takes place is independent of their individual wills. Indeed the result of the competitive struggle is often contrary to that willed. The struggle is a result of the operation of laws of the capitalist mode of production.

Engels cites the example of another law of capitalism, the existence of a mass of unemployed workers, which he, and Marx after him, called the industrial reserve army. Here too the members of this army are not unemployed by choice. It is true that the existence of unemployed can be consciously wished by the capitalist class. But the usefulness of such an army to them is a consequence of their being capitalists. Their class interests exist objectively and their consciousness merely reflects this class interest.

Here is Marx's discussion in *Capital* of the consequences of the operation of the law:

> The law that always equilibrates the relative surplus population, or industrial reserve army, . . . this law rivets the laborer to capital more firmly than the wedges of Vulcan did Prometheus to the rock. It establishes an accumulation of misery, corresponding with accumulation of capital. Accumulation of wealth at one pole is, therefore, at the same time, accumulation of misery, agony of toil, slavery, ignorance, brutality, mental degradation, at the opposite pole, i.e., on the side of the class that produces *its own product in the form of capital.*

Engels cited this entire passage in SUS^3 and Suvin, so eager to build his case against Engels, cites the last sentence as part of another argument without ever informing the reader that the words were not those of Engels but of Marx. Although it may take us off the main line of our discussion here, it is important for what follows to consider this matter in more detail. Suvin gave as an example of crassly mechanical materialism Engels' comparison of the capitalist accumulation of riches on the one pole and of misery, degradation, and so on at the other pole of society with the accumulation of hydrogen and oxygen at the positive and negative poles during water dialysis. Throughout his essay, Suvin constantly seeks to find differences between Marx and Engels. And it is therefore important to note that it was Marx who used the term *poles* in the excerpt from *Capital* cited above. The oppositions associated with the term poles are quite clearly borrowed from the physics of magnetism and/or electric charge. Hence if such a comparison is to be labeled crassly mechanistic then Marx is just as guilty as Engels. But Suvin is apparently unable to recognize the operation of dialectical processes in nature and associates mechanism with any process in the natural sciences. In taking refuge in Marx, he conveniently overlooks the numerous instances where Marx clearly expressed his views on the applicability of dialectics to nature, such as, for example, his characterization of the dialectical method as "the method of dealing with matter."[4] In essence, Suvin generates his own discrepancies in the parallelism between the natural and social world: Nature is mechanistic, society is dialectical, and as we shall soon see, he regards nature as materialistic and relegates society to the realm of the ideal.

Let us continue with Engels' further examples of the conflicts in the capitalist mode of production. Engels describes another dialectical process connected with business crises which again does not depend on individual will:

> The circulation of commodities is, for the time being, stopped. Money, the means of circulation, becomes a hindrance to circulation. All the laws of production and circulation of commodities are turned upside down. The economic collision has reached its apogee. *The mode of production is in rebellion against the mode of exchange.* (p. 142)

Let us cite one more example from Engels:

> Whilst the capitalist mode of production more and more completely transforms the great majority of the population into proletarians, it creates the power which, under penalty of its own

> destruction, is forced to accomplish this revolution. (p. 146)

Here we see an example of the Marxist understanding of social consciousness in the materialist conception of history. The laws of social development lead to conditions of social being which give rise to specific forms of social consciousness. The viewpoint expressed here represents the fundamental Marxist position on the relationship of thinking to being. The conditions of social being give rise to social consciousness, in this case, to revolutionary consciousness. The development of this revolutionary consciousness is necessary to give rise to the next stage of social development, which Engels describes as follows:

> *The proletariat seizes political power and turns the means of production into state property.* (p. 146)

Thus the social development which emerges from the conflict described above is a clear demonstration of the operation of dialectical processes in society, and how Suvin can describe it as "crassly mechanical" is beyond all imagination. Equally baseless, as we have already seen, is Suvin's seeking refuge in Marx for his attack on historical materialism. To make this point more clearly, we can turn to the same dialectical logic used by Marx in *Capital*:

> Along with the constantly diminishing number of the magnates of capital, who usurp and monopolise all advantages of this process of transformation, grows the mass of misery, oppression, slavery, degradation, exploitation; but with this too grows the revolt of the working class, a class always increasing in numbers, and disciplined, united, organized by the very mechanism of the process of capitalist production itself. The monopoly of capital becomes a fetter upon the mode of production, which has sprung up and flourished along with, and under it. Centralisation of the means of production and socialisation of labor at last reach a point where they become incompatible with their capitalist integument. This integument is burst asunder. The

> knell of capitalist private property sounds. The expropriators are expropriated.
>
> The capitalist mode of appropriation, the result of the capitalist mode of production, produces capitalist private property. This is the first negation of individual private property, as founded on the labor of the proprietor. But capitalist production begets, with the inexorability of a law of Nature, its own negation. It is the negation of negation.[5]

This brief selection from *Capital* follows the same pattern of dialectical analysis used by Engels in the examples above. Suvin, in calling this approach crassly mechanistic, simply confuses law-governed phenomena with mechanism.

In rejecting historical materialism, Suvin proposes what is essentially a modified form of utopian socialism: "a synthesis of the bold, vertical *utopian will to revolution* and the careful, horizontal *knowledge of preconditions for revolution*." In rejecting historical materialism, Suvin rejects class struggle as the base on which revolutionary consciousness develops. Nor is it surprising that Suvin does not indicate what he regards as the preconditions for revolution, for the preconditions for revolution emerge from the particular form that the class struggle takes in a given country. Marx and Engels recognized that capitalism itself creates the working class which, under penalty of its own destruction, is forced to accomplish the revolution. They recognized the need of the working class to form its own organizations to defend the interests of the workers' side in the class struggle. Thus the conditions of class conflict give rise to proletarian consciousness and to proletarian organizations. Marx and Engels devoted considerable energy to helping form such organizations and to strengthening the revolutionary content of their programs. Lacking from Suvin's "utopian will to revolution" and "knowledge of the preconditions for revolution" are the material means for expression of this will and the material means for carrying out such revolution, a lack which is reflected in Suvin's attack on the materialist content of scientific socialism. "[T]heory also becomes a material force as soon as it has gripped the masses," wrote Marx.[6] And it is the revolutionary organizations of the working class that are the material expression of this revolutionary theory. This dialectical connection between the ideal and the material is missing from Suvin's approach.

In his *Philosophical Notebooks*, Lenin again and again stressed that the essence of dialectics is the law of the unity and struggle of opposites. Historical materialism sees the class struggle as the main manifestation of the dialectical process in class societies. Many socialist-minded petty-bourgeois intellectuals find it difficult to see a class struggle that is waged primarily by the working class as the key to their own liberation. For such recognition would require acceptance of the priority nature of the struggle waged on the main battleground of class conflict, the terrain of the industrial core of the working class, a terrain where the average petty-bourgeois intellectual feels the least comfortable, but nevertheless a terrain where the proletariat is best organized and potentially able to mount the most militant and disciplined struggle.

Suvin's inability to see the relevance of Engels' *Socialism: Utopian and Scientific* to the situation today appears to be directly connected with his inability to accept the working class and the class struggle as the leading factors in the revolutionary struggle for socialism.

NOTES

1. Darko Suvin, "'Utopian and Scientific': Two attributes for Socialism from Engels," *Minnesota Review*, NS6 (Spring 1976), pp. 59-69.
2. Frederick Engels, *Socialism: Utopian and Scientific*. Page references are from the third volume of Karl Marx and Frederick Engels, *Selected Works* (Moscow: Progress Publishers, 1970).
3. *Ibid.*, p. 141.
4. Karl Marx, *Letters to Kugelmann* (New York: International, 1934), p. 113; letter dated June 27, 1870.
5. Karl Marx, *Capital, 1* (New York: International, 1975), p. 763.
6. Karl Marx and Frederick Engels, *Collected Works, 3* (New York: International, 1975), p. 182.

DISCUSSION

Comment from the floor: In this paper we heard an answer to the question raised earlier of whether we can talk about a petty bourgeoisie and to the comments that the American working class is so submerged in the bourgeoisie that there is no working class at all. Just as Engels points out that the bourgeoisie, independently of the will of its individual members, represents the interests of the bourgeois class, there exists a working class independently of the individuals' recognition of their own status as workers, even if some think of themselves as part of the middle class. Therefore, we have an answer to the question of whether we can talk about a working class in modern technological society.

Comment from the floor: You have analyzed Suvin's criticism of comparison of the iron laws which link up the actions of humans to the actions of atoms, molecules and so on. What you have done is to have formally refuted his categories, internally. I don't know that you have refuted what seems to be at the heart of his analysis, which is: If Marxism is so scientific, how do we account for the fact that the proletariat does not respond according to this structure of capitalism? In other words, can Marxism be saved if we say that it is a science?

Reply: Suvin did not actually raise these questions, although Lenin did deal with them. He formulated what he called the Law of Revolution regarding the conditions that are necessary for a revolutionary crisis to exist and the necessary conditions for a revolution to actually take place. In doing so he dealt with the question of the subjective factor, the consciousness. But Suvin did not talk about that. That's another discussion.

Comment from the floor: You do not seem to hit some points Suvin is trying to make. First of all there is the basic problem of whether the dialectics of nature has any sense at all. You say that he is quoting Marx through Engels. I think the intention is to criticize them both, not just Engels. If dialectics is lost, so is Marxism. And therefore it is very important to discuss this question in such a way as to make dialectics acceptable to theoreticians in general, to philosophers, because this is a basic philosophical point. Bringing into the question problems of magnetism and plus and minus is a little bit superficial, I would say.

Reply: But it is Suvin who was being superficial. He did not discuss. He simply declared that it is mechanistic to say that there are opposite poles and consequently it is mechanistic to compare society to the natural world. He did not discuss the question; he did not really criticize. He merely asserted that if a polarity exists in nature it is not dialectical, but mechanistic. But there was no discussion. Is there a dialectics of nature? I would say yes and perhaps we should have a paper on that. But many people simply attack Marxism by making Engels the bad one for having imposed dialectics on nature.

PUBLIC SPHERE, LABOR, AND INTERACTION:
A Methodological Critique of Jürgen Habermas' Social Theory

Robert Holub
Wigand Lange
Sara Markham Pietsch
Stephen Pietsch
Charles Spencer
Ronald Young
University of Wisconsin

Jürgen Habermas is one of the most influential and prolific New Left theorists in West Germany today. His philosophical and political views, based heavily on the "critical theory" developed by the Frankfurt School, have been important to the New Left since the middle '60s when receptivity to anti-establishment theory was at its peak. His influence on the student movement until 1968 was considerable, and even after many leftists criticized the "practical Habermas" for his characterization of elements among the students as "left fascist," the "theoretical Habermas" continued to gain adherents in intellectual circles. It is not difficult to understand why. Habermas is one of the most capable and articulate theorists expressing New Left trends. His utilization of revised Marxist categories, his intertwining of Western sociological, psychological and political thought with pseudo-revolutionary critique, his call for a return to a "critical" social theory based on Hegel's dialectic, as well as the complexity and linguistic intricacy of his style have provided worn-out bourgeois and retreating leftist scholars with a haven for their theoretical speculations.

But Habermas' influence is by no means restricted to his actual written works or to the West German intellectual. As editor of the prestigious *Wissenschaftliche Reihe* (Scientific series) of the Suhrkamp Press, Habermas has access to the decision-making power over the publications of the most important liberal-progressive publishing house in West Germany. As one of the directors of the Max Planck Institute, an important research center in the Federal Republic, he can exert considerable influence over the direction and ideological content of social-science research. Perhaps more significant for our consideration is the interest Habermas has sparked in New Left circles in the United States. Several of his longer works have been translated into English and his essays have appeared frequently in various American journals. With Habermas, therefore, we are dealing with neither an ephemeral nor a local phenomenon, and his importance for young social scholars both here and abroad cannot be ignored.

Because of the diversity and complexity of Habermas' theoretical concerns it is impossible to undertake a critique of all his works in this limited space. Instead we have chosen to concentrate on specific concepts which have been focal points for his development in the '60s. The thrust of our discussion will therefore emphasize two essential areas of Habermas' thought: first, his methodological approach to problems of capitalist society as it is reflected in the development of his conceptual framework; and second, his position vis-a-vis the tradition of Marxist thought, his borrowings, distortions and modifications of established Marxist concepts. The following investigation should thus serve to uncover some of the central theoretical and political trappings of Habermas' system and their relation to the broader current of New Left thought.

1. *The Public Sphere*

Habermas' first important contribution to the New Left came with his concept of the *public sphere* (*Öffentlichkeit*). The most concise discussion of this term may be found in Habermas' entry in the 1964 edition of the *Fischer Lexikon: Staat und Politik* (State and politics) in an article entitled simply "Public Sphere."[1] The publication date is significant, for in the 1964 edition of the lexicon the central concept of Jürgen Habermas' book *Strukturwandel der*

Öffentlichkeit (The structural transformation of the public sphere) made its debut in the vocabulary of political science. Like many of his contemporaries, Habermas felt the need to introduce new terminology or to redefine established terms with a new content. Although a greatly condensed version of the book, the article gives a convenient text for examining the method by which the term *public sphere* is derived and justified. Secondly, this text provides a starting point for discussing the problem of terminology in general. In Negt and Kluge's treatment of the question of a "proletarian model" for cultural "revolution," for example, Habermas' premises are criticized, but the term *public sphere* is accepted as a valid one based on Habermas' arguments.[2] With the introduction of the term into the English language the question of the relationship of terminology to a system of theory as a whole emerges, particularly as it applies to the vast literature stimulated by and reflecting the language and terms of Marxism.

It should be noted that Habermas was hardly unique in his concern for such matters as public sphere, publicity, public relations and public opinion in the '60s. Indeed, his focus was not unlike that of other West German intellectuals who criticized manipulative and ideological features of control by institutions in capitalist society and who called for democratization through critical public discussion. Analyses of the mass media, the discussions of the "consciousness industry," a term popularized from the writings of Adorno and Horkheimer, the student protest against the reactionary and powerful Springer Press, and the numerous attempts to establish counter-media illustrated this trend in the Federal Republic. While offering some positive elements of critique when seen in the light of the preceding '50s, these New Left analyses and actions were limited by certain theoretical and practical weaknesses. Since the early '70s the New Left has been criticized for the subjectivity of its critical approach, its lack of attention to the real problems of the working class and its idealistic alternatives, which were often co-opted by the bourgeoisie. The alternatives propagated by Habermas and others were often drawn from the traditions of the German enlightenment; ideals of the ascendant bourgeoisie such as public sphere, reason, tolerance and critique were directly adapted by intellectuals in late capitalism for purposes of contemporary social criticism without employing a materialist historical approach. Habermas' work on the public sphere canonized this intellectual trend in the '60s to reappropriate eighteenth-century ideals in support of a critical stance. Fundamental change was believed to be possible through change in ideas and the means of their dispersal; thus the existing economic relations were never seriously called into question.

Habermas' concept of a public sphere is both a symptom of and an impetus to these emerging tendencies in the '60s. It describes a realm of assembled private individuals in which public opinion about matters of general interest is formed and freedom of assembly and association is guaranteed. The concept of public sphere and public opinion arose in the eighteenth century during a "specific phase" of bourgeois development. In the Middle Ages the public sphere had served merely to "represent" the power of the nobility and the church. In the eighteenth century, however, with the emergence of national and territorial states and the rise of the exchange of commodities and information, a polarization between the public authorities of the state (the parliamentary, military, and bureaucratic apparatus) and the bourgeois public sphere of private individuals took place. This public body of individuals without political office arose from the bourgeois family structure, assumed first a literary, then a political function in which the public discussion focused on the activities of the state. The public sphere served as a mediator between state and society, and its crucial role was to raise criticism through public opinion concerning the "ruling structure organized in the form of the state,"[3] that is, the feudal authorities in the eighteenth century. Today, in what Habermas calls the "social welfare state of mass democracies," he sees instead of the eighteenth-century separation of the bourgeois public sphere and public authorities an interweaving of the two spheres; the liberal model is thus no longer appropriate, and the idea of the public sphere "threatens to disintegrate with the structural transformation of the public sphere itself."[4] This disintegration is caused by the intrusion of special competitive interests of large organizations, which in effect close the public sphere, weaken its critical function, and depoliticize it. The state, according to Habermas, is presently no longer subject to reason. He calls then for a rationalization through public discussion of public authorities among private individuals. The bourgeois public sphere could only be realized today as a "rational reorganization of social and political powers under the mutual control of rival organizations committed to the public sphere in their internal structure as well as in their relations with the state and each other."[5]

The inadequacies of Habermas' usage of the term *public*

sphere are most evident in his methodological approach to the problem. In the preface to his book *Strukturwandel der Öffentlichkeit* Habermas claims that his type of historical sociological approach allows him "greater discretion in the face of historical material."[6] With this statement Habermas dismisses the necessity to consider the existence of such a sphere and the extent to which this sphere was actually "public." It should be noted that Habermas is here reacting against traditional bourgeois empirical method. Yet, why should Habermas assume that empirical data and verification and the "equally severe criteria of a structural analysis"[7] are mutually exclusive, and not complementary procedures? Indeed, it is difficult to envision a really thoroughgoing analysis of a societal phenomenon which would not meet the demands of logical, structural, and empirical validity. By approaching the problem with this method, however, Habermas gives himself free hand to select sources, facts, and data which substantiate his conclusion. Before beginning his discussion he has already assumed that the public sphere has historical and sociological, if not empirical, validity. It is no wonder that the examples which he cites for empirical verification are selected to support his contentions. By relieving himself of the rigors of a complete historical analysis of the ideal of the public sphere, Habermas has fallen into the methodological trap of proving his presupposition.

In fact, one could contend with some justification that Habermas' inability to escape this vicious methodological circle stems from his failure to define the public sphere as a part of bourgeois ideology, that is, as an ideal necessary first for the struggle against feudalism and later as an apology for bourgeois domination. Like the realm of reason, which Engels correctly labels as nothing more than the idealistic realm of the bourgeoisie,[8] the public sphere discloses more about bourgeois consciousness than about the society from which it arises. Habermas' acceptance of this ideal as a real expression of societal relationships leads him, like all historians of ideas, away from the totality of society which he seeks to investigate and forces him to play down the role of class struggle in the conception and propagation of the ideal. Thus the ownership of the means of communication, the class backgrounds and interests of "contributors" to the public sphere, and the actual content of the writings of these "contributors" are of secondary importance. The public sphere according to Habermas is endowed with its own internal dialectic, only mediated by structural alterations in the composition and development of its propagators, the bourgeoisie. The error here is therefore twofold: Not only does

Habermas fail to describe the concept of public sphere as the ideology of the ruling class and to explore the material basis for this ideology, but also he confuses the forms of bourgeois hegemony and the manner in which the bourgeois ideology is itself dispersed with the content of that ideology and the control of the organs of communication.

Habermas' central methodological failing therefore involves the manner in which he arrives at the public sphere as a viable consideration for analysis. In this respect it is noteworthy that the fact that the public sphere is an "ideal" or "model" is mentioned in the book *Strukturwandel der Öffentlichkeit,* but is totally ignored in the shorter lexicon entry. The absence of such a clarification may lead the naive reader to believe that the public sphere as defined by Habermas actually existed at some point in the development of the bourgeoisie. A glance at the history of the eighteenth and nineteenth centuries demonstrates, however, that this was not the case in England, Habermas' model case, nor on the continent, the "variants" to the English model. Wolfgang Jäger, for example, in his book *Öffentlichkeit und Parlamentarismus* has shown that Habermas' contentions have little basis in English history. Rather, Jäger contends, the actual ideal which Habermas attributes to his liberal public sphere is more aptly suited to the bourgeoisie of the 1848 parliament in Germany. There, and not in the more advanced capitalist nation of England, where interest groups exerted political influence through parliamentary and extra-parliamentary organizations, one finds the expression of the "stylized" public sphere which Habermas claims as paradigmatic. Significant for the underdeveloped German bourgeoisie of the early nineteenth century, however, is the fact that, in contrast to England, it contained relatively few representatives from industry and commerce; that is, that the ideal of a bourgeois public sphere in Habermas' definition has its roots and fullest development in the inability of this class to secure political domination through its economic position.[9]

It should be noted in this respect that Habermas arrives at the notion of public sphere through an incorrect utilization of abstraction. Abstraction itself, of course, is not objectionable. After all, Marx too made use of abstractions to uncover the mechanisms of capitalist political economy. Rather it is the methodological application of the principle of abstraction which is objectionable here. For, unlike Marx, Habermas does not begin with concrete social reality, but with an ideal propagated by the intelligentsia of a specific class (the bourgeoisie) under specific historical circumstances (the struggle against feudalism). Once this concept has been established, however, it is made into a concrete object for analysis, projected backwards into Greece and forwards into the twentieth century, and implicitly established as the measure of freedom and reason in a given society. Some of the implications of this methodoloy have been explored in the preceding paragraphs. What is important to notice here is that Habermas utilizes a decidedly unhistorical method despite the wealth of historical material which he advances to support his contentions. The ideals of the bourgeoisie become for him the parameters of reality, and all other social systems, including the late stages of capitalist society, are measured against them.

To illustrate these general criticisms of Habermas' unhistorical approach, we will examine a specific example of the tendency to substitute ideals from the history of ideas for the realities of past and present social problems. In his reconstruction of the eighteenth-century concept of the public sphere as a structure in which the social and political changes are accomplished through "discussion," Habermas tends to repeat the mistakes of eighteenth-century thinkers who viewed society from the perspective of one of its parts, instead of as a totality. For example, Habermas mentions casually a "plebeian sphere" and then only as a "variant" of the bourgeois public sphere. The social implications involved in the fact that, as Habermas says, this plebeian sphere was "to some extent suppressed" receive no treatment. The tendency to equate society as a whole with "bourgeois society" without differentiating the various social classes and sectors of society is a major fault in Habermas' theory, especially when specific social problems are discussed.

The problem of referring to a plebeian sphere as a "variant" of the dominant public sphere becomes clearer when Habermas applies the eighteenth-century model to the nineteenth century. Habermas' plebeian sphere refers in part to Robespierre's activities, the Chartist movement of the British working class and the anarchist movement. Only vaguely does Habermas refer to the continental workers' movement. These developments, reflecting the conflict of material interests of social classes, are dismissed as "ephemeral" and "illiterate." As Mattenklott and Jäger have pointed out, the social upheavals of the nineteenth century express the interests not only of day-laborers, but also those of the petty bourgeoisie, who voiced opposition against the feudal counter-revolution and against the betrayals of the liberal bourgeoisie.[10]

Habermas' neglect of the so-called variants to the bourgeois public sphere is more than just an oversight. His model rests upon the supposition that societal conflicts are reconciled through the mediation of the public sphere and not resolved through class conflict. Mattenklott writes:

> The plebeian public sphere in Robespierre's time was in fact not a variant of the liberal public sphere. Rather, it appeared politically at the historical moment when it became obvious that the liberal bourgeoisie was neither capable of nor willing to extend the realization of bourgeois rights of freedom to all levels of the middle class and to the middle and small farmers.[11]

Even if consideration is limited to the English model of the public sphere, Habermas' neglect of the very real existence of non-parliamentary opinion-making processes, such as labor strikes and demonstrations,[12] makes his reconstruction of a model one-sided. Habermas chooses to ignore the part played by the liberal bourgeoisie in suppressing opposition. He insists on the peripheral character of everything but the public sphere and reduces conflicting class interests to variants of a liberal model. By this method Habermas considers and legitimizes solely bourgeois social consciousness and ideology.

In his reconstruction of the eighteenth-century European conceptualization of the public sphere, Habermas premises this "mediating" function ascribed to this sphere by eighteenth-century thinkers:

> The public sphere as a sphere which mediates between society and state, in which the public organizes itself as the bearer of public opinion, accords with the principle of the public sphere — that principle of public information which once had to be fought for against the arcane policies of monarchies and which since that time has made possible the democratic control of state activities.[13]

The fallacy of this structural conceptualization lies in the separation of society from the state with the premise of the public sphere as the mediation between them. What is attributed to the public sphere is actually a matter of social relations and the development of society itself. Habermas defines three mediating factors within the public sphere: 1) public opinion, 2) the public, which is the bearer or mediator of public opinion and 3) the process of publicizing.

These factors presuppose certain historical developments. In order for the bourgeoisie to oppose the social consciousness promoted by the feudal order, it must first develop an intelligentsia as part of society to formulate and disseminate its own ideology. Secondly, the bourgeoisie must develop an ideology and a program which appeals to more than its own narrow interests in order to gain the support of other classes. This requires not merely an abstract sphere of public influence, but the actual historical development of social sectors whose interests do not objectively correspond to those of the feudal order. For the process of "publicizing" to occur, the historical development of the means and instruments of communication are a precondition, and the bourgeoisie must have property relations permitting use and ownership of these means and instruments.

In applying the model to present-day society, the assumption of a mediating function of the liberal public sphere is applied to the conditions of late capitalism in order to posit an "interweaving of the private and public realm." From this premise of a loss of the primary function of mediation through interweaving, Habermas concludes that the idea of the public sphere is to "threaten to disintegrate."[14] Had Habermas focused upon the essential material conditions and relations and their historical development, he would have seen this "threat to disintegrate" as the necessary outcome of capitalist relations, which dominate the instruments and mode of communication in the same way that they dominate the means and mode of production in general.

2. *Labor and Interaction*

In our observations concerning Habermas' concept of the public sphere, we have attempted to show how his approach to historical phenomena prevents him from a materialist analysis. His dealings with modern capitalist society demonstrate some of the same weaknesses. Again one finds the lack of concern for empirical validity and a neglect of practical application. It is not coincidental therefore that Habermas himself considers his essays in *Technology and Science as "Ideology,"* for example, to be "experimental" and "occasional works" which seek to accomplish nothing more than to "define some premises" and to "suggest consequences."[15] Indeed, Habermas recognizes the limitations of this approach to social phenomena, but dismisses them as unimportant. What matters to him is the establishment of a theoretical framework within which general abstractions can be accommodated. The introductory statement to the essay "Technology and Science as 'Ideology'" evidences this approach:

> I am proposing an interpretative scheme that, in the format of an essay, can be introduced but not seriously validated with regard to its utility. The historical generalizations thus serve only to clarify this scheme and are no substitute for its scientific substantiation.[16]

This separation of the "interpretative scheme" and the "historical generalizations" from "utility" and "scientific substantiation" is again the result of a methodological approach which attempts to oppose an empirical analysis with a radical interdisciplinary structural model. The pitfalls of such a method for a Marxist analysis will be the subject of the following discussion of Habermas' categories of labor and interaction.

Habermas' development and exposition of the categories of labor and interaction come during the middle '60s in three central essays: "Labor and Interaction: Remarks on Hegel's Jena Philosophy of Mind," "Technology and Science as 'Ideology'" and in the discussion of Marx in *Knowledge and Human Interest*.[17] These categories are particularly important for an understanding of Habermas since they represent his attempt to come to terms with the philosophical traditions of Marxism and to find theoretical tools with which to analyze recent developments in capitalism. Indeed, one can assert that these concepts are simultaneously the basis of his critique of Marx and the foundation for his later theoretical development.

In light of Marx's discussion of labor and the production process, Habermas' definition of labor takes on particular significance. In an attempt to arrive at terminology which accounts for all of human history, he assigns labor the following definition:

> By "work" or *purposive-rational action* I understand either instrumental action or rational choice or their conjunction. Instrumental action is governed by *technical rules* based on empirical knowledge. In every case they imply conditional predictions about observable events, physical or social. These predictions can prove correct or incorrect.[18]

There are two significant aspects of this definition: first, the attempt to establish a more general category of labor than has hitherto existed in the Marxist tradition, and second, the heavy reliance on science and technology as an integral part of labor in the abstract. Both deserve further consideration.

In terms of methodology, Habermas' abstraction of labor represents the endeavor to go beyond Marx's usage of the term. By widening the conceptual framework of this category, however, Habermas has had to disregard the basis of the category of abstract labor in capitalist society, i.e., the creation of value. What remains is only the form of labor, the "instrumental action" and the "rational choice"; the content of the category, the value-creating force in capitalist society is eliminated by the formal definition. No doubt Habermas feels that on the basis of modern capitalist production this type of widening is necessary and that his definition supersedes the "particular" notion of labor developed by Marx in the nineteenth century. What he has done, in fact, is to redefine the category on an anthropological basis without considering the historical conditions of which this category is a product. Habermas seeks Marx's support for his new definition by citing those passages in *Capital* where Marx talks explicitly about the labor process as such, as a relationship between man and nature, thus choosing to ignore Marx's emphasis in *Capital* and elsewhere on the social determinants of labor and production. Erich Hahn has pointed to this methodological error in his discussion of Habermas' basic categories: "The basic mistake seems to be that Habermas tacitly assigns to the category of labor in Marx's theoretical system functions which only the category of 'social production' can fulfill, and that he holds up man's interaction (*Auseinandersetzung*) with nature as a natural being as the basis of historical materialism."[19] This generalizing of the category of labor thus returns social theory to its pre-Marxist stages, to the anthropological premises of philosophy of the early nineteenth century.

The second aspect of Habermas' definition of labor, its emphasis on science and technology, is logically related to his widening of the category. Indeed, one of the obvious functions of labor in Habermas' sense is that it tries to account for changes in the relative importance of the development of technologies which were not as evident in the nineteenth century. Central to this redefinition is thus Habermas' discussion of the role of technology as defined in *Theory and Practice*. In this book he undertakes a revision of the labor theory of value, asserting that science and technology have become the primary force in generating value (including surplus value); compared to technology, human labor as the creator of value, has become increasingly unimportant. Again Habermas goes to Marx for theoretical support for this thesis. Basing his contention on the following passage from the *Grundrisse*, Habermas claims that Marx too recognized the role of technology in creating value:

> ... to the degree that large industry develops, the creation of real wealth comes to depend less on the labour time and on the amount of labour employed than on the power of the agencies set in motion during the labour time, whose "powerful effectiveness" is itself in turn out of all porportion to the direct labour time spent on their production, but depends rather on the general state of science and on the progress of technology, or the application of this science to production.

Whereas Marx refers explicitly to the creation of wealth, Habermas reads into this the creation of surplus value. Marx said further:

> ... labour time ceases and must cease to be its measure (wealth) ... exchange value must cease to be the measure of use value.... [Capitalism] on the one side ... calls to life all the powers of science and of nature ... in order to make the creation of wealth independent of the labour time employed on it. On the other side, it wants to use labour time as the measuring rod for the giant social forces thereby created, and to confine them within the limits required to maintain the already created value as value. Forces of production and social relations ... appear to ca-

> pital as mere means, and are merely means for it to produce on its limited foundation. In fact, however, they are the material conditions to blow this foundation sky-high.[20]

What characterizes the economy under late capitalism is the contradiction between enormous creation of real wealth through the development of the forces of production and the necessity of capitalism to keep the production of wealth in the restrictive form of commodity production. The revision of the labor theory of value enables Habermas to remove this primary contradiction from late capitalism.

Once the value-creating function of technology is removed from Habermas' definition, however, the entire category collapses, and one is left with labor, both physical *and mental*, as the sole creator of value. By offering no support for his contentions other than this misreading of Marx, Habermas has himself undercut the category which he attempts to define and has demonstrated again his tenuous relationship to Marx's entire theory of political economy.

One notices similar tendencies in Habermas' discussion of interaction, the other half of this category pair. Although Habermas often refers to it simply as the "institutional framework," the more complete definition in "Science and Technology as 'Ideology'" discloses that he has in mind much more than institutions in their usual sense:

> By interaction . . . I understand *communicative action*, symbolic interaction. It is governed by binding *consensual* norms, which define reciprocal expectations about behavior and which must be understood and recognized by at least two acting subjects. Social norms are enforced through sanctions. Their meaning is objectified in ordinary language communication. While the validity of technical rules and strategies depends on that of empirically true or analytically correct propositions, the validity of social norms is grounded only in the intersubjectivity of the general understanding of intentions and secured by the general recognition of obligations.[21]

Again it is evident that Habermas has undertaken the widening of

Marx's category, that of social relations or relationships of production. But here too he has abstracted away from the concrete historical determinants in order to reach a more general formulation. The class nature of societal organization and "interaction," the property relationships which underlie the form and content of "communicative" and "symbolic" action, are obfuscated by the suggestion that norms and "consensual" and "reciprocal." We are once more confronted with an anthropological schema which in its abstraction covers rather than reveals the real determinants of social behavior.

In this respect, it is significant that Habermas uses as his starting point the reference to "at least two acting subjects." The approach to the definition of this category is thus not unlike the approach of early bourgeois economists to the category of production. Like Adam Smith and Ricardo, who regarded "the solitary and isolated hunter or fisherman,"[22] as the starting point for the analysis of political economy, Habermas uses the simplest relationship between two individuals as the basis for interaction. Marx's critique of his predecessors is equally applicable here. For the isolated interpersonal relationship, like the isolated individual, is not the starting point of history but rather the historical result. To be sure Habermas' category attains a certain degree of universality through this abstraction, but only through the sacrifice of its historical dimension. Methodologically, Habermas is again falling behind Marx in his attempt to go beyond him.

The thrust of Habermas' definition of interaction, however, is categorized not only by his abstracting from an ahistorical relationship, but also by his attempt to subsume under this term dimensions traditionally assigned to the realm of ideology or consciousness. While his category of labor can be "empirically" or "analytically" validated, interaction attains a validity "only in the intersubjectivity of the mutual understanding of intentions." The ideology which propagates certain social norms and its real interests, and the individual consciousness which assimilates these norms, are radically separated in order to maintain the facade of consensus. The control of "outer nature" through the labor process and the control over "inner nature" through the institutional framework are viewed as mutually exclusive processes, the latter being emancipated only by "an organization of social relations that is bound to communication free from domination."[23] The unity of class domination and class ideology is thus distorted through a subjective consideration of the roots and ramifications of interaction. Only in this way can Habermas contend that "the institutionalized relation of force that establishes the distribution of the instruments of production is based on a structure of symbolic interaction."[24] The consequences of the idealist methodology in observing interaction thus lead Habermas to the typical idealist formulation, which views ideology as primary and property relationships as secondary.

In considering "labor" and "interaction" we have dealt with each as a separate entity in order to illuminate some of the methodological problems with these categories from a Marxist perspective. It should be noted that this treatment does no violence to Habermas' system since he himself views the developments of "labor" and "interaction" as distinct, or at best vaguely related. In fact, Habermas' theory of crisis in modern society is based on the contention that the "rationalization" of interaction has not kept pace with the "rationalization" of labor. Under the technocracy found in late capitalism the systems of purposive rational action predominate, actively adapt with the goal of totally rationalizing production, in the process turning humans into perfectly controllable machines. The institutional framework, on the other hand, only adapts passively to the requirements of "labor," and the disproportion between these two developments results in crisis.

> A new conflict zone, in place of the virtualized class antagonism and apart from the disparity conflicts at the margin of the system, can only emerge where advanced capitalist society has to immunize itself, by depoliticizing the masses of the population, against the questioning of its technocratic background ideology: in the public sphere administered through the mass media.[25]

Habermas replaces class struggle here by "politically effective discussion":[26] "In the last analysis the process of translation between science and politics is related to public opinion."[27] Even though in a highly industrialized society rational discussion will have to be led by experts, Habermas insists that it "can proceed only from the horizon of communicating citizens themselves and must be led back to it."[28]

That Habermas has neither a definite addressee for the enlightenment which the opening of the public sphere should propagate, nor a practical means for implementing this enlightenment, represent two obvious shortcomings of his model. This, however, is merely another reflection of his inability to relate concrete property relationships of the capitalist system to the suppression of the very opening of the public sphere which he calls for.

It should have been evident in our discussion of labor and interaction that these categories are adopted from the Marxist terminology: forces and relationships of production. It is also obvious that Habermas' fundamental error in dealing with these concepts — i.e., abstracting from them and reestablishing them on an anthropological basis — lies in the severing of their dialectical unity, as it exists in Marxist theory. For Marx the development of the forces of production in contradiction to the relationships of production brings about a crisis situation necessitating revolutionary change. The ramifications of Habermas' separation of these two categories therefore go beyond his own theoretical model and its methodological trappings; there are practical implications as well. For if the central contradiction of capitalist development is no longer the basis for a revolutionary program, if capitalism itself is no longer viewed as a system of production which must be overcome, then practice becomes either utopian or a means to perpetuate the hegemony of the ruling class.

3. Technology and Social Evolution

After separating the categories of labor and interaction, Habermas faced the dilemma of developing an analytical system which could reconcile their "inherent" separation. This is the focus of his later works, *Legitimationsprobleme in Spätkapitalismus* (Legitimacy problems in late capitalism) and *Zur Rekonstruktion des Historischen Materialismus* (Toward the reconstruction of historical materialism).[29] It is obvious that in order for a society to maintain itself, a fairly regular, harmonious and productive relationship must prevail between societal labor and interaction. If conflicts of interest or other antagonisms arise that disturb or destroy the harmonious collaboration of social labor and interaction, a society's existence could become threatened. But if, like oil and water, labor and interaction represent essentially separate entities, there is no assurance that without the intervention of some mitigating factor, the developing interests of social interaction and socially necessary labor will not come into irreconcilable contradiction. At such a point, society would surely suffer a breakdown.

In his studies on legitimation, Habermas attempts to broach the problem just outlined by deriving more concrete, workable concepts from his abstract categories *labor* and *interaction*. His concept of interaction leads him to the idea of the socio-cultural sector.[30] In the socio-cultural sector, through speaking and acting in a social context, individuals develop the cognitive systems with which they understand themselves and the world. From labor, Habermas derives the economic sector. In the economic sector, production and the relations involved in production are organized. For handling the task of integrating and maintaining the harmonious, productive functioning of the economic and socio-cultural sectors, Habermas asserts the existence of a political sector which takes the dominant position between the other two sectors.[31]

In Habermas' analysis, when the three sectors develop in an interdependent, harmonious way, a functioning societal system arises. Within this societal system, the political sector assumes the function of leadership and the maintenance of systemic competence and integration in a changing world. If within all sectors the prevailing normative consensus is that the entire societal system is functioning harmoniously, then the system is said to be legitimate. Leadership is assisted in its quest to maintain systemic integration and guidance by the propagation of a justification system which upholds systemic legitimacy and which is closely tied to societal cognitive systems, e.g., myth, religion, ideology.[32] For Habermas, legitimacy and societal integration are not predicated upon static conditions, but are ultimately confirmed as a societal system undergoes change.

In Habermas' view, while pressures for change in societal systems may originate somehow exogenous to the system or within its socio-cultural sector, the greatest impetus for change arises from the technological advance of productive forces. The pressures for social evolution that accompany qualitative change in technology and productive forces bring with them a crisis of legitimacy. For example, Galileo's telescope brought the cosmology and cognitive abilities of Catholicism into question, while the productive potential of the capitalist factory system challenged the capacity of the household crafts industry to meet society's demands for commodities.

Habermas asserts that if a societal system is to overcome the challenge of technological advance, and weather its legitimacy storm, it must alter its societal form in order to accommodate the orderly integration of new production and cognitive systems. He measures a society's ability to overcome crisis by the extent to which it can develop a learning process for the management of orderly change.[33] In Habermas' system, as a societal entity makes the necessary adjustments to technological change, it evolves through a series of stages.

Habermas identifies the stages of social evolution roughly as 1) pre-high culture, 2) traditional, 3) modern, 4) post modern.[34] Evolution in cognitive systems proceeds from myth and magic, through religions of revelation, systematic religions, to philosophy and to ideology.[35] In general, changes in political organization occur as well. In effect, Habermas posits that there exists an ideal relationship between technological advance and societal evolution which is positive and linear. (See Figure 1.)

Figure 1

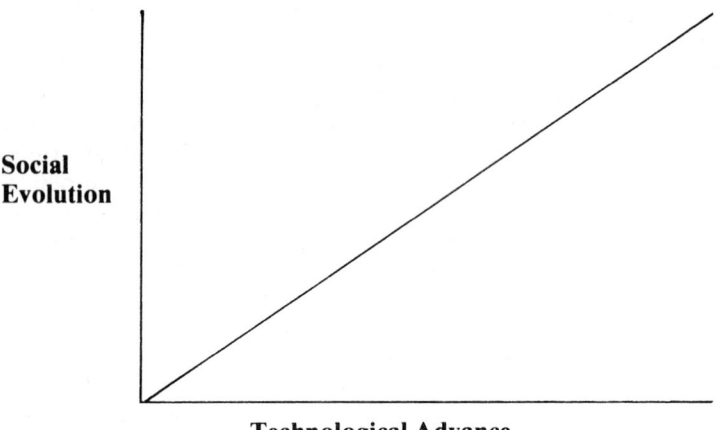

Social Evolution

Technological Advance

Successful societies are those which are able to move along the line. But, since a societal system's movement along the line of the optimum relation between technological advance and social evolution is precipitated by crisis, Habermas attributes deviations below the line to the particular inability of a societal system to respond to its crisis with the proper learning process. He views deviation below the line as merely a "regression" from the optimum evolutionary course.[36]

Implicit in Habermas' evolutionary ideas is the tacit argument that optimal societal evolution is accompanied by an extension of participation in the political sector to ever broader elements of society. For example, the rule of aristocratic classes gives way to parliamentary governments composed of the elected representatives of enfranchised voters. As the franchise widens, the base of popular involvement in the political sector broadens. Until the present crisis of late capitalism, a broad electorate has in part created the base of legitimacy for liberal democracy in capitalist society.

Stripped of its peculiar jargon, however, Habermas' model nearly parallels the developmental model popular with many bourgeois social scientists in the '50s and '60s.[37] If the term *modernization* is substituted for technological advance, and if the term *democracy* is substituted for social evolution and public participation in the political sector, the two models nearly match. In his understanding of the developmental relationship between technology and societal evolution, Habermas merely reproduces, with characteristic flourishes, bourgeois social theory in a New Left jargon.

Not until his treatment of the legitimacy crisis of late capitalism does the extent of Habermas' adherence to the latest developments in bourgeois social science become unclear. In order to explain the inability of modern societies to meet the challenge of rapid technological advance — ecological destruction, the arms race, etc. — as they restrict public access to the political process, some Western social scientists have posited a curvilinear relationship between modernization and democracy.[38] (See Figures 2 and 3.)

Figure 2

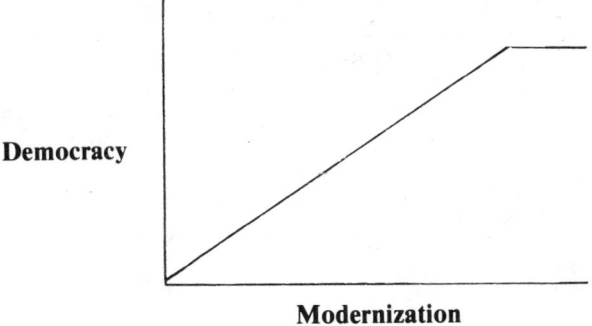

Figure 3

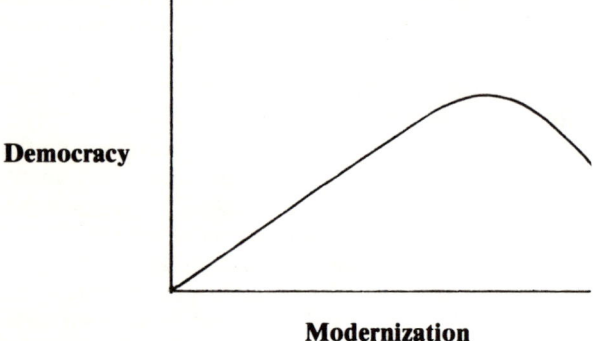

Of course, these analysts tend to equate democracy with its bourgeois parliamentary form. They equate the historical limitations of bourgeois parliamentary democracy in particular with the historical limits of democracy in general. Whereas they correctly identify the historical limitations of bourgeois forms of democratic organization, they appear to fail to understand the need for radical transformation of democratic organization.

Habermas, on the other hand, refuses even to recognize that present capitalist forms of democratic organization have reached their historical limits. He seems to insist that deviations below the line of optimal societal evolution in modern Western cases merely represent their failure to use public discussion in the quest to solve their problems. His legitimacy studies invariably conclude with a call to revive public discussion.

NOTES

1. This article was reprinted in the collection of essays *Kultur und Kritik* (Frankfurt am Main: Suhrkamp Verlag, 1973), pp. 61-69. An English translation appeared in *New German Critique* (Fall 1974), pp. 49-55. All of our English quotes concerning the public sphere are taken from this translation unless otherwise indicated.
2. Oskar Negt/Alexander Kluge, *Öffentlichkeit und Erahrung. Zur Organisationsanalyse von bürgerlicher und proletarischer Öffentlichkeit* (Frankfurt am Main: Suhrkamp, Verlag, 1972).
3. Jürgen Habermas, "The Public Sphere: An Encyclopedia Article (1964)" in *New German Critique*, 3 (Fall, 1974), p. 49.
4. *Ibid.*, p. 55.
5. *Ibid.*
6. Jürgen Habermas, *Strukturwandel der Öffentlichkeit. Untersuchungen zu einer Kategorie der bürgerlichen Gesellschaft* (Neuwied and Berlin: Luchterhand, 6 ed., 1974), p. 8.
7. *Ibid.*
8. Marx/Engels, *Werke* 20 (Berlin: Dietz, 1973), p. 17.
9. Wolfgang Jäger, *Öffentlichkeit und Parlamentarismus. Eine Kritik an Jürgen Habermas* (Stuttgart: Kohlhammer, 1973).
10. *Ibid.*, p. 22; Gert Mattenklott and Klaus Scherpe, eds., *Westberliner Projekt: Grundkurs 18. Jarhhundert (Analysen)* (Kronberg-TS.: Scriptor, 1974), p. 47.
11. Mattenklott/Scherpe, *op. cit.*, p. 47.
12. Jäger, *op. cit.*, p. 22.
13. Habermas, "The Public Sphere," p. 55.
14. *Ibid.*, p. 55.
15. Jürgen Habermas, *Technik und Wissenschaft als 'Ideologie'* (Frankfurt am Main: Suhrkamp Verlag, 1968), p. 7.
16. Jürgen Habermas, "Technology and Science as 'Ideology,'" *Toward A Rational Society, Student Protest, Science, and Politics* (London: Heinemann Educational, 1971), p. 90.
17. "Labor and Interaction: Remarks on Hegel's Jena *Philosophy of Mind*" in Jürgen Habermas, *Theory and Practice* (Boston: Beacon, 1973), pp. 142-169; "Technology and Science as 'Ideology'" in Habermas, *Toward a Rational Society*, pp. 81-122; Habermas, *Knowledge and Human Interest* (Boston: Beacon, 1971).
18. *Toward a Rational Society*, p. 91f.
19. Erich Hahn, "Die theoretischen Grundlagen der Soziologie von Jürgen Habermas," Heinrich von Heiseler *et al.*, ed., *Die "Frankfurter Schule" im Lichte des Marxismus* (Frankfurt am Main: Verlag Marxistische Blaetter, 1970), p. 74.
20. Karl Marx, *Grundrisse* (New York: Vintage, 1973), pp. 704-706. For further discussion see Peter Laska, "A Note on Habermas and the Labor Theory of Value," *New German Critique*, 3 (Fall, 1974), pp. 154-162.

21. *Toward a Rational Society*, p. 92.
22. Karl Marx, "Introduction to A Critique of Political Economy," in *The German Ideology* (New York: International, 1970), p. 124.
23. Jürgen Habermas, *Knowledge and Human Interest* (Boston: Beacon Press, 1971), p. 53.
24. *Ibid.*, p. 328.
25. *Toward A Rational Society*, p. 120.
26. *Ibid.*, p. 61.
27. *Ibid.*, p. 74.
28. *Ibid.*
29. Jürgen Habermas, *Zur Rekonstruktion des Historischen Materialismus* (Frankfurt am Main: Suhrkamp Verlag, 1976).
30. Jürgen Habermas, *Legitimationsprobleme im Spaetkapitalismus* (Frankfurt am Main, 1973), p. 14ff.
31. *Ibid.*, p. 15.
32. *Ibid.*, p. 23.
33. *Ibid.*, p. 27.
34. *Ibid.*, p. 31.
35. *Ibid.*, p. 23.
36. *Ibid.*, p. 24.
37. See Seymour Lipset/R. Bendix, *Social Mobility* (Berkeley: University of California Press, 1959); Marion J. Levy, *Modernization and the Structure of Societies* (Princeton: Princeton University Press, 1966).
38. Robert W. Jackman, *Politics and Social Equality* (New York: Wiley, 1975); Juillermo O'Donnell, *Modernization and Bureaucratic Authoritarianism* (Berkeley: Institute for International Studies, 1973).

DISCUSSION

Question from the floor: Could you elaborate a little bit more on the idea of inner nature?

Reply: Inner nature is basically our psychological makeup. This is where the New Left brings in its attempt to accommodate Freudian psychology and Marxism. One can say that no matter what happens you are still a psychological being and you will have to figure things out that way.

Habermas defines production as production of the truth, and he divides that into two branches: (1) the history of truth, which is the history of science or of the control of outer nature by natural science and technology, while the force behind these is the mind or inventiveness; and (2) the history of norms or values and ideas. So you have technology developing on the one hand and ideas and philosophy on the other, the latter being connected to inner nature.

Question: But which does he say is primary?

Reply: He says the two are separate; they are autonomous. He says, for example, that the administration of the state sector has to be kept separate from the legitimization process in the public sphere. If they are not kept separate, the state as a public authority will have to begin exposing the workings of the economy. He is often quite frank about economic contradictions; he speaks frankly of surplus value being produced. If the state sector with its involvement in the economy becomes involved in legitimization processes, this will endanger the exposure of exploitation by means of surplus value.

He seems to assert that the mind is primary, that the intellectual class is primary and is driving things forward, but if you try to pin him down, he says there is interdependence. But he can do that only by denying it where they both come together, namely in production. He separates them there, and then, later on, says that they are interdependent. He says that the basis-superstructure model is no longer valid.

He often says that "while Marx was fine for the nineteenth century, this is no longer the case in the twentieth century and that is why I am developing this new terminology to deal with it, because certain things in Marx are inadequate, although I will pick up some of the things he said." This is why Habermas can be so attractive to certain groups. Habermas says that what we need are many other streams of thought: psychology, bourgeois sociology, and political science.

NEW LEFT THEORIES ON
THE MODE OF PRODUCTION

Domenico Sindico
University of Minnesota

In the recent New Left literature dealing with developing countries it is constantly argued that the specific nature of their development makes it impossible to integrate this process in the preexisting models of analysis. This approach is particularly important in relation to the concepts of *mode of production* and *economic formation of society*. It is therefore important to carefully analyze the meaning, use and misuse of these concepts in order to cut through the confusion that currently prevails in scholarship on these topics.

In the first place the concept of *specific nature* is basically unclear and often confused with the concept of *uniqueness*. The two concepts are, in fact, very distinct. *Specific* makes sense only in relation to *general*; in other words the concept can be understood only as part of a more general one; on the other hand, *uniqueness* assumes an autonomous existence. To consider, say, the feudal mode of production in China or Latin America as being unique implies difficulties in relating this concept to the more general one of the *feudal mode of production*. These difficulties explain the proliferation of new terms such as the *colonial mode of production*.[1] On the other hand, the *specific nature* of the Chinese or Latin American feudal mode of production should only assume recognition of particular conditions in the practical application of the general concept to the particular, *specific* situation.

This distinction is particularly necessary in order to clarify the concepts of *mode of production* and *economic formation of the society* without falling into vulgar simplifications (everything is different, therefore everything is specific) or demagogical declarations (the specific characteristics of every nation, region, city, village, household).

According to the above considerations *specific nature* is a concept that can be used to recognize some particular aspect within a given general category. It is impossible for such a concept (*specific nature*) to create new categories because it does not have autonomous existence outside of the general category from which it receives its own essence. Therefore if we use this definition as a basis of analysis of a particular reality, we have a concept that, on one hand, will let us analyze different experiences in their particularity, and, on the other hand, will enable us to insert these experiences into a larger framework, without depriving them of their autonomy. The importance of this result is particularly evident when we need to check general concepts and interpretations against concrete experiences. The relation that we can establish between *specific* and *general* is therefore similar to that between *genus* and *species*.

On this base, the discussion about mode of production in developing countries can be carried out within the framework of the concepts described above. From this point of view to consider circumstances in every country as unique and *sui generis* is a vulgar empiricism.[2] There is no doubt that the circumstances in every country which we decide to analyze will be unique; what is important is to point out that the particularity of such circumstances does not imply the creation of a conceptualization *sui generis* that will reflect these characteristics.

A critique of the idea that the *specific nature* of non-European countries cannot be reduced to a Marxist model of analysis is now necessary, since Marx's analysis cannot be restricted to the European and Mediterranean world. Therefore the application of the same categories of analysis and periodization to other continents would not be "Eurocentric," since the *specific nature* of a society, in a Marxist analysis, cannot be reduced to the Weberian dimension of historical contingency. A deeper analysis, in accordance with our definitions and without denying the specific characteristics of any particular historical development, must take into consideration the basic elements that make it possible for us to analyze a historical process. In Marxist terms these elements are the social relations of production which cannot be combined in an arbitrary number of ways, and therefore, even if they appear under different forms, cannot always create new class relations according to the particular history of each village, city or region.

To continuously propose new terminology or to attempt to create new *modes of production*, such as a *colonial mode of production*, seems very much a *deus ex machina* which is dangerous, since it keeps us away from the fundamental problem, which is to analyze the specific aspects of a particular situation on the basis of the knowledge and with the analytical tools available at a given moment.

Therefore the fact that other societies have been classified in analogy to Europe is not a theoretical problem; what is important to study is the usefulness of this classification and the way the specific features of other societies are or are not in contradiction with this definition.

An interesting concept is presented by Dhoquois, who very clearly presents the relation between the concept of a mode of production and any concrete situation:

> Once given the general kind, it is then possible to specify concretely its regional varieties through the geographical and historical varieties. Every incarnation of the mode of production includes structural and conjunctural particularities which complicate enormously and sometimes even hide the general kind which is always invisible and present.[3]

Other authors consider that the coexistence and interaction of different modes of production within a given society determine the specific character of the dominant mode of production in such a society.[4]

The real difficulty is in the application of the general concept to the particular case; the problem, therefore, does not arise from irreducibility but from complications connected with lack of precise knowledge as regards the economic mechanisms functioning in the particular societies in question.

Another clarification of terms is now necessary. We are concerned with the definition and distinction of the concept of *mode of production* and of *economic formation of the society*. First of all the German expression used by Marx, *Ökonomische Gesellschaftsformation*, should be translated *economic formation of the society* and not *socio-economic formation* as it is usually translated. In the

German text, *Ökonomische* is the only adjective; it modifies and characterizes the second term *Gesellschaftsformation*. It is therefore incorrect to add a second adjective *socio* that does not appear in the original. If we add the term *socio* we are diminishing the strength of the first term *economic* and moreover including a new variable in the basic characteristics that define the concept. If we use the term *economic formation of the society* we are defining a particular analytical unity, the society, observed from a precise point of view, namely, the economic. On the other hand the term *socio-economic formation* does not clearly define this analytical unity and moreover includes two elements, the economic and the social, as forming a basis for the concept. From the analytical point of view, the phrase *economic formation of the society* more correctly reflects the original terminology. This is not a purely philological problem, but one of fundamental importance, since it conveys a distinct meaning of the concept *Ökonomische Gesellschaftsformation* and affects its subsequent application.

Our task is now to examine the relation between the mode of production and the economic formation of the society. A common thesis in recent New Left literature is that the economic formation of the society is the concrete application of the abstract concept *mode of production* to a given society.[5]

Althusser considers the mode of production as the interrelation between an economic basis and 1) a legal and political entity; and 2) an ideological entity. He considers the economic formation of the society (which he calls *economic and social formation*) to be a structure:

> resulting from the combination of at least two modes of production, one of which is dominant and the other subordinated. . . . This combination of several modes of production . . . produces specific effects that explain the particular form of the legal and political superstructure, and of the ideological superstructure.[6]

This quote is important since the idea of the coexistence of different modes of production inside the same society appears in the work of several authors. Now, while we accept this concept, we have yet to analyze the relationship between *mode of production* and *economic formation of the society*.

As regards this particular problem, Bartra observes that the concept of mode of production and of economic formation of the society must be analyzed in their concrete reality and not at an abstract level:

> the mode of production is the concrete synthesis of multiple determinants, that permits an explanation of the particularity as well as the generalities of an economic formation. The concept of economic formation, if it is understood as the combination of various modes and forms of production, does not constitute a concept that represents a greater concreteness, since this concreteness is expressed in the dominant mode of production. The concept of economic formation of the society expresses a global reality through a greater dissociation of the terms of the synthesis *particular-general*; for this reason the concept makes us recognize the historical and logical links of the parts to the whole. It permits the location of the determined particularities, by means of the generality, and the recognition of the condition of generalization of the particularities of the different social forms.[7]

This formulation is very convincing, and we want to point out that Bartra considers the relation of the mode of production to the economic formation of the society as a relation of *genus* to *specie*, with emphasis on the concrete aspect of these concepts, and does not consider the mode of production as an abstract category, useful only as an analytical tool.

With regard to the definition of the term *mode of production*, we tend to look at the whole work of Marx, and not simply any one particular passage, so that we see a mode of production determined by the relations existing among the elements constituting the infrastructure of a society, namely the dialectical relationship between the relations of production and the productive forces. In this sense, it is wrong to consider the exchange of commodities as a determinant element of a mode of production. For example, in order to have commerce as a consequence of a capitalist structure of a given society, the geographic dimension of the exchange is not important, but the fundamental aspect resides in the intrinsic quality of the product which is exchanged: the commodity in which labor, the source of surplus value, is incorporated.[8] In this sense, analyses such as those made by Gunder Frank profoundly distort the

Marxist concept of mode of production.[9] In conclusion the mode of production represents a typical, but concrete and real, moment of the development of the forces of production.

Sereni presents a particularly good definition of the concept of the economic formation of the society in which he includes superstructural as well as infrastructural elements, in a unity formed around the dominant mode of production.[10] In the concept *economic formation of the society* the term *economic* must be understood in the Leninist sense, that is, without excluding, but, on the contrary, enriching itself dialectically with extra-economic elements, which fully realize the Marxist concept of economic.

The reevaluation of the economic formation of the society as a category of analysis becomes therefore important in reaffirming the role of superstructural elements in contrast to the strict economism typical of the Second International, against which Lenin himself had to struggle.

From the viewpoint of historical materialism the concept of economic formation of society can be the starting point for any historical analysis; this is because any assumption is valid only insofar as it is based on reality. We therefore have to start any analysis with a concrete structure, in this case a particular society, and then study its development.

Concluding these considerations we think of the categories of mode of production and economic formation of society as two concepts, which serve as bases for historical analysis from the perspective of historical materialism. These concepts cannot be considered true or false, since a concept cannot serve as a base for making a true-false judgement but is only capable of explanation in relation to the analysis of a given reality. Its importance, therefore, can only be judged in relation to its capacity to permit the interpretation of a given concrete reality.

For the Marxist researcher, this relation between scientific analysis and concrete reality is the indispensable parameter necessary for evaluating the meaning of any particular work. A concept therefore can provide a framework for the analysis, but it could never be a substitute for it.

NOTES

1. This concept can be found in Ciro F.S. Cardoso, "Los modos de producción coloniales: estudio de la cuestión y perspectivas teóricas" in *Historia y Sociedad*, No. 5, Spring 1975.
2. I agree, therefore, with José F. Ocampo, "On what's new and what's old in the theory of imperialism," *Latin American Perspectives*, 2 (Spring 1975).
3. G. Dhoquois, "La formación económico-social como combinación de modos de producción" in Sereni, Glucksmann, Godelier and others, *La categoría de formación económica y social* (Mexico: Ed. Roca, 1973), p. 130. Translations are my own throughout.
4. Among them Althusser and Bartra.
5. Among them Gallissot and Labica.
6. Cited in Pierre Beaucage, "¿Modos de producción articulados o lucha de classe?" in *Historia y Sociedad*, No. 5, Spring 1975.
7. Roger Bartra, "Sobre la articulación de modos de producción en América Latina" in *Historia y Sociedad*, No. 5, Spring 1975.
8. Karl Marx, *El Capital. Libro I. Cap. VI* (Mexico: Siglo XXI, 1971).
9. Andre Gunder Frank, *Capitalism and Underdevelopment in Latin America* (Harmondsworth, England: Penguin Books, 1971).
10. Sereni, Glucksmann, Godelier and others, *La categoría de formación económica y social* (Mexico: Ed. Roca, 1973).

DISCUSSION

Comment from the floor: If I understand what you are doing, you are criticizing the application of what we call dependency theory, for instance, the kind of analysis we find in Gunder Frank suggesting that it is impossible to speak of feudalism in Latin America, for any economic units that exist are functioning in relation to the capitalist system.

Reply: There is no doubt that this paper is directed at Gunder Frank, particularly in regard to Latin America. He says that Latin America has never been feudal because it was encircled immediately by a capitalist system. He assumes that feudalism means a restricted market as in the manorial system in Europe, and that in Latin America there is no manorial system, so you cannot assert that it is feudal. If we look at Marx, it is the relations of production that determine whether or not a system is feudal. If you take a model, such as the mode of production, abstractly, you say: "This is true, therefore it must apply everywhere or nowhere." But this is a mistake, because a model is never true or false. You take a model and if you have a concrete situation, you check one against the other and ask whether or not the model helps in the analysis.

Comment from the floor: To assert that there has never been feudalism in Latin America is historically wrong. Even bourgeois historiography has shown that the Spaniards imposed traditional Spanish feudal relations on South America, especially Chile.

Comment from the floor: I think it is time that we had some discussion among Marxists on the whole concept of the use of models and paradigms in scientific analysis, because a model basically is an idealization of the objective reality. Almost by definition, a model is approximate and partial and can never be complete. I do not think that the materialist conception of history is a model. It does not make that kind of abstraction from reality that, say, a mathematical model makes (or similar models in physics or social science, for that matter) where you set up a system of axioms which you then use to develop properties by means of formal logic. Use of a model in this way is not consistent with any kind of dialectical analysis.

Reply: I would agree that a model is not a final way of describing society. It is useful as a tool. Even Marxists have used models. It is important to understand what people are doing with their use of models and how they are being used. Marxists use models to analyze ideology, but not to idealize.

SCIENCE & SOCIETY

―――――Vol. XLI, No. 3――――――FALL, 1977――――――

ON CONTRADICTION IN DIALECTICAL MATERIALISM
M. Mark Mussachia

THE SPHERE OF PRODUCTION AND THE ANALYSIS OF
CRISIS IN CAPITALISM *John Weeks*

THE SOCIAL RELATIONS OF SCIENCE MOVEMENT (SRS)
AND J.B.S. HALDANE *Robert E. Filner*

THE MUDFISH AND THE CROCODILE: UNDERDEVELOPMENT
OF A WEST AFRICAN BOURGEOISIE *Susan B. Kaplow*

STATUTEN DES KOMMUNISTEN KLUBS IN NEW YORK *Philip S. Foner*

SOCIALISM OR CAPITALISM IN THE USSR? *Al Szymanski*

BOOK REVIEWS **BOOK NOTES**

Subscription: $ 8 Foreign subscription: $ 9
Institutions: $11 Foreign institutions: $12

SCIENCE & SOCIETY, 445 West 59th Street, New York, New York 10019